Tastes From the Temple

Kitchen Witchery from the Temple of Witchcraft

by

Dawn Hunt
and the Temple of Witchcraft
Community

Kathy — Happy Cooking + Many Blessings

COPPER CAULDRON PUBLISHING

Credits

Primary Writing & Compilation: Dawn Hunt
Contributions: The Temple of Witchcraft community
Cover Photos: Kari Weidenburner
Layout & Publishing: Steve Kenson

For more information visit:
www.coppercauldronpublishing.com
www.templeofwitchcraft.org
ISBN 978-0-9827743-2-8, First Printing
Printed in the U.S.A.

Thank you from the bottom of my heart:

To Justin, for unconditional love, support, laughter, and promising to eat whatever I cook.

To Kari Weidenburner for your friendship, always believing in me and your killer photography skills.

To Christopher Penczack, Steve Kenson, and Adam Sartwell for taking a chance on me.

To Alix Wright for late night tea and great advice.

To Justina Burnett for assistance, and fabulous hair.

To Kevin Sartoris for long talks, valuable insight, and shameless promotion.

To my Temple family, especially Matooka, Wren, Silver, Wes, Lisa, Bonnie, Rama, Jocelyn, and all who contributed to this book: I hope you love it and that I have done you proud.

Table of Contents

Foreword

I find it ironic the one person in our household who doesn't really cook is writing the forward to the Temple of Witchcraft's community cookbook, *Tastes from the Temple*. But growing up with an old-fashioned Italian mother, I learned to appreciate food from an early age. Good food was at every occasion, but the special occasions – holidays, birthdays and family gatherings, our food was particularly special. My Mom would make all sorts of special treats everyone loved. That continued onward when we both converted from Catholicism to Witchcraft, and would host massive public Samhain rituals with parties afterward blessed with her amazing holiday food. Sadly, I never got her passion for cooking and fortunately ended up with partners who are great cooks, but I did retain my passion for enjoying good food, particularly around celebrations and holidays.

Though my Mom has passed from this world to the realm of the ancestors, the growing "family" of the Temple of Witchcraft keeps our community well-fed. It was at one of our leadership retreats that our Aquarius minister, Lisa, came up with the seed that would sprout to become this fundraising book. Traditional Pagan potlucks are hit-or-miss at most gatherings I've attended, but she noted how good the food was at this particular gathering and that generally we're blessed with a good feast after our Sabbats, lovingly arranged by our Cancer ministry, which oversees all things motherly and care-taking, including the kitchen. She suggested we do a cookbook as a fundraiser, so we put out the call for submissions.

The project languished for a bit, as we were all putting together other projects for the Temple, ranging from new classes and public rituals to our first ever summer festival gathering, TempleFest. None of us had ever put together a cookbook before. It was only when our dear friend Dawn Hunt

—known far as wide as "the Kitchen Witch"—got involved that the project took on a life of its own. Dawn has been tremendously supportive of our work in the Temple: vending and teaching at our events, often preparing magnificent feasts for both Temple rituals and for major personal events hosted by Temple members. In fact, in a very magickal full circle, she prepared the funeral feast for my mother's crossing rite, held in the same ritual space and home where all those Samhain parties happened. Her love of cooking and sharing food with others reminds me so much of my Mom, who was really the spiritual mother to the Temple of Witchcraft, supporting the unofficial community of gathered friends, students, and seekers for so many years. Food and magick truly go hand in hand, bringing us together. And they both understand that deep truth.

It is with that passion that Dawn has gathered, organized and contributed her own writings and recipes to the magickal volume you now hold in your hands. Use it to gather *your* own community, to share with your family, friends, coven, circle, and grove. Let it inspire you to make food with magick and to make magick with food. You won't be disappointed.

Blessings,

Christopher Penczak
Nov 2, 2011

Introduction

I have been a Kitchen Witch my whole life. The path is not something you choose, it is something you discover. Like a favorite scarf hidden under the bed for years that you just happen to stumble across while cleaning one day. When I casually picked up a book on Kitchen Witchery while trying to kill time in a bookstore, a light bulb went off. I finally had a name for the magickal and spiritual work that had been part of my life for so long. In 2007, I volunteered to give a workshop on Food Magick at a local Beltane festival and I have been doing it ever since!

A couple of years ago, I was asked to give a workshop at a festival in Peterborough, NH, called Celebrate Samhain. At the time I was still living in New York and planning on moving to New England in the coming year. Early in the day I made small talk with a gentleman about the kilt he was wearing and didn't think much of it. I had heard the award-winning author Christopher Penczack was going to be at this same event. In all honesty, I knew his name but had not read any of his books at that point. Little did I know the sweet man I had chatted with about his kilt was the admired man everyone was talking about!

I was flattered and honored when asked to participate in the evening's closing ritual. Having never played such an important role before was a bit intimidating. Christopher stood across from me in the center of the circle as we called the elements in for ritual. It was at that point I started to giggle and laugh uncontrollably and Christopher right along with me. We were instant friends and my world has not been the same since.

When my husband, Justin, and I finally made the move from New York to New England the process of settling in took some time. We really didn't know anyone or have a sense of the community. But when Beltane came along I just had to get out and dance and sing and celebrate even though I didn't know where to go. A friend mentioned the Temple of Witchcraft was holding a Beltane ritual. Remembering how much fun I had with Christopher at that Samhain ritual, I decided to don my flower wreath and the (now infamous) burgundy dress, and head out to dance the maypole.

The welcome and love I felt the moment I walked in the door was overwhelming. Here I was, a stranger from out of town, who had only met a handful of the seventy-some people in attendance for moments many months ago. Yet, I was greeted with hugs and bright smiles. Warmth and gratitude for my presence was in every hug I received, even the people who I had never met before said things like "Oh, aren't you 'the Kitchen Witch'? We love you! So happy to have you join us!" I was overwhelmed and still am to this day by the people in the Temple of Witchcraft. From that moment on I have done anything they have ever asked of me! Which, sometimes, means losing sleep and working too much, but I am sure everyone in the Temple would have the same story and the same feeling: it is always worth it!

Just a few months later, after the very first TempleFest, I was asked to work on this project. Since what I love most is bring people together around food, I was ecstatic to help make this book come to life. When you see what it is people eat, love to eat, and why, you get to know them in a way. I learned a lot about the people who helped contribute to this book. I learned about their families, their traditions, and what they love to share with people closest to them. Like a pot-luck feast, this cookbook has a little bit of everything and something for everyone. This collection of recipes is not like ones you have seen before. Each recipe tells a story and comes with some magickal information. Roll up your sleeves, break out your apron, and enjoy all the Tastes of the Temple!

Blessed be!
Dawn Hunt

Chapter 1:
Comfort Foods

"Food, like a loving touch or a glimpse of
divine power, has the ability to comfort"

– Norman Kolpas

What are "comfort foods" exactly? Most people's minds immediately run toward mashed potatoes, chicken soup or macaroni and cheese. Comfort foods are, I think, one of the most magical types of foods. These dishes warm the heart and make us feel like we are receiving a big hug from the inside.

Once again, the magick of these foods comes from the intention put into them. Think about how you feel when you are sick and your nose is running. All you want is a nice bowl of soup. (As I write this there is a huge pot of chicken soup simmering on my stove. I happen to have caught as pretty bad cold.) As you are preparing that soup you stir it thinking, "I know this soup is going to fix me right up" or "This is just what I need to put me right". This is a great example of Kitchen Magic. You are already putting into the food the outcome you want to receive. It is no wonder we crave hearty, comforting foods when we are feeling like we need a pick me up. Not only do they have robust, tasty ingredients, but they are filled with the intention of joy and comfort.

Comfort foods have a way of bringing us back to a place where we are safe and loved. They remind us of home. It is funny to think how a slice of toast covered in honey has a way of chasing away the feeling that I seem to be catching a cough. How many of us turn to a scoop of chocolate ice cream to ease a broken heart? It is important to note that just because some of these foods make us feel better emotionally when we are down or sick, because so many of them are rich, high-calorie foods, you may want to modify them to suite your dietary needs. Keeping in mind that once in a while, full fat, high calorie foods can be just what the soul needs!

So, the next time you could use a little culinary snuggle, try one of these recipes. Just remember your intention is everything here!

Chapter One: Comfort Foods

Chicken Soup (a kitchen witch's cure-all)

This is one of my very own recipes that has taken years to perfect. To be honest, my mom never really made chicken soup (other than from a can). Sad but true. I didn't really know the wonder of homemade chicken soup until I developed an allergy to MSG, found in so many condensed soups. I thought "well, what kind of kitchen witch am I if I don't even have my own chicken soup recipe?" So here you go: Easy, wonderful, delicious and full of feel-better power. Couple that with a night of watching your favorite movies and you will be right as rain in 24 hours!

Ingredients

2 Tablespoons Cucina Aurora Rosemary and Oregano Oil (or plain olive oil)

2 boneless, skinless chicken cutlets cut into bite size pieces

1 large onion, chopped fine

3 cloves garlic, minced

3 ribs celery, diced

3 medium carrots, chopped

2 32 oz. containers organic chicken broth

2 Tablespoons fresh chopped sage

1/4 cup fresh parsley, chopped (or 2 Tablespoons dried parsley)

1/4 cup fresh rosemary (or 2 Tablespoons dried rosemary)

Sea salt and ground black pepper to taste

Directions

In a large sauce pot, heat olive oil on medium-high heat. Add onions, garlic, and celery. Cook, stirring until onions and celery begin to soften; about 5 minutes. Add chicken. Cook, stirring, until chicken is no longer pink. Add carrots, broth, sage, parsley, rosemary, sea salt and pepper. Stir well. Cover and reduce heat to a simmer. Let simmer 1–4 hours. Serve hot with noodles, rice, wild rice, or crusty Italian bread for dipping.

Magickal Notes

Chicken soup is good for the body and the soul. We should eat it when we are not sick to keep us well, but most of us don't. Not only is this age old remedy the go-to for moms across the world when their kids are sick, but the ingredients hold true magickal properties. When combined with the right intentions of health and wellness they form this powerful potion. Chicken holds the power of good health, onions banish negativity and illness, garlic protects us from evil or negativity, carrots keep us grounded, and rosemary has tremendous healing properties. You can see how these foods, on their own, can aid in healing, and good health. Together they are all but unstoppable!

Chapter One: Comfort Foods

Marvelous Meatloaf

I was quite surprised when we were looking for recipes for this collection, when we asked for comfort foods we did *not* get bombarded with eight hundred recipes for meatloaf. It seems one of those foods we all remember our moms making on a cold autumn night. It shows up on menus of restaurants claiming to have "home cooking" or "just like mom used to make" and remains a popular dish in so many homes. So, why didn't we get any recipes for it? Well, maybe it was just so I could share mine with you!

In the first year of marriage to my husband, when the weather turned cold I surprised him with one of my favorite meals, meatloaf, mashed potatoes, and green beans. He was not impressed. He smiled and went along with it because I was so excited and, like the wonderful man he is, he didn't want to hurt my feelings. He ate every morsel on his plate and went back for more. After dinner he confided in me that meatloaf was one of his most loathed dinners and yet he simply *loved* the one I made for him. I still to this day do not know what is so special about my meatloaf, but I have not found a better one yet!

Ingredients

1 package (1 lb.) meatloaf mix – beef, pork, veal

1 egg

1/2 cup bread crumbs

1/4 cup mustard

1/3 cup ketchup

1 Tablespoon dried parsley

1 Tablespoon dried chopped onions (or Cucina Aurora Onion Dip Mix)

1 teaspoon garlic powder

1 teaspoon soy sauce

1 teaspoon Worcestershire sauce
Salt and pepper to taste
1/2 cup ketchup & 1/4 cup mustard for top

Directions

Heat oven to 375 degrees. In a large bowl kneed together meat, egg, bread crumbs, 1/4 cup mustard, 1/3 cup ketchup, parsley, onions, garlic powder, soy sauce, Worcestershire sauce, and salt and pepper. In a large oven safe casserole dish, shape meat mixture into a loaf. Mix 1/2 cup ketchup and 1/4 cup mustard together and cover the top and side of the meatloaf with it to form a sort of glaze. Bake for 40-50 minutes or until center is no longer pink. Slice and serve warm with mashed or baked potatoes.

Magickal Notes

This is one of those meals that fills you up body and soul. When done right, magickally, this recipe can solidify friendships. Beef (and veal) are both kinship foods. The pork in the mix adds wealth and prosperity to that kinship energy. Therefore combining the two grows and stabilizes friendships and family bonds. The most important thing with this recipe is to kneed the meat mixture by hand. It sounds a bit gross but you must touch the meat mixture and put your energy in with your own hands. Feel the mixture between your fingers and see how you are shaping your relationships with love and joy in your heart.

Traditional Winter Stew

Now here is a recipe I grew up on. My father is a hunter. He loved to go away every year in mid-November to upstate New York and go deer hunting. I think for the most part it was my Dad, in his quiet way, who planted the roots of loving nature in my heart. When I was little we would go up in the woods together. We would walk, softly in the woods hunting small game (but never really shooting at anything). He would always tell me how important it was to be thankful to the animals for giving their lives so we could eat. I was taught there is little to no waste when it comes to deer hunting done properly. Dad would tan the hide, we would eat the meat, he would keep the bones for tools and things like that. We would talk about the circle of life and how to respect nature for all her bounty. Dad's deer hunting trips always fell on my birthday and so the first pot of venison stew was usually close to Thanksgiving. Mom would put it on the stove in the morning and by evening we would feast on tender meat and crusty bread. But it is just as good with beef since venison may be a bit hard to come by.

Ingredients

1 lb. stew meat (beef or venison)

1 cup flour (or Gluten Free flour)

2 Tablespoons olive oil

1 large onion chopped fine

3 cloves garlic minced

2 stalks celery chopped fine

2 carrots sliced

2-3 potatoes cut into small cubes

1 large parsnip cut into small cubes

4 cups organic beef broth

1 Tablespoon each rosemary, sage & parsley

Salt & pepper to taste

2 teaspoons Worcestershire sauce

Directions

Dredge meat with flour. In a large sauce pot heat oil. Cook dredged meat in pot until browned on all sides. When meat has browned, add onions, garlic, celery, and carrots. Let cook, stirring about 5 minutes. Put all remaining ingredients in pot and let simmer for 2-3 hours or until meat is tender. Stir occasionally. For thicker stew, simmer with lid off, for thinner stew simmer with lid on. Serve with crusty bread or cornmeal biscuits.

Magickal Notes

Nothing says comfort like a bowl of hot stew on a cold night. Remember to stir this thick stew clockwise for protective energy. When adding the herbs, envision comfort to all who eat it. Imagine wrapping your loved ones in a warm blanket close to a bright fire. As you wait for the stew to simmer down, turn off the lights and take a moment to light a candle in the dark. Meditate on the light and enjoy the darkness. See how this small flame brings so much light to the darkness. Your meal will be the light and comfort to the hungry souls of those who will eat it!

Four Cheese Baked Macaroni

Whenever I ask one of my classes what comes to mind when I say "comfort foods" at least half of the crowd shouts out "Macaroni and Cheese!" What is it about Macaroni and Cheese that fills the holes in our hearts when we have had a terrible day? So many of us live on the bright orange stuff that comes from that blue box when we are in college. It is a favorite of children everywhere and yet we never ever seem to get sick of Mac and Cheese! This recipe is a bit more grown up, with four flavorful cheeses baked together into bubbly heaven.

Ingredients

1 lb. uncooked elbow macaroni

2 cups low fat milk

2 Tablespoons flour

1 cup shredded sharp cheddar cheese

1/2 cup shredded Gouda cheese

1/2 cup shredded Gruyere cheese (or baby Swiss)

1/4 cup grated Romano cheese

1 teaspoon dried mustard powder

Pinch cayenne pepper

1 teaspoon salt

1 teaspoon ground black pepper

1 8oz. package frozen chopped broccoli (thawed and drained)

1 cup Panko bread crumbs

Directions

Heat oven to 350 degrees. Coat a large oven safe baking dish with nonstick cooking spray. Cook pasta to package instructions, drain and return to pot. While pasta is cooking, in a medium sauce pan combine milk and flour and whisk over medium heat until it is smooth and comes to a soft boil. Lower heat to lowest setting and whisk in cheddar cheese, Gouda, and Gruyere until smooth. Remove from heat and whisk in Romano cheese, dried mustard powder, cayenne pepper, salt and pepper. Stir cheese sauce into warm drained pasta. Gently fold in chopped broccoli. Spoon mixture into prepared baking dish. Sprinkle the top with Panko bread crumbs. Bake, uncovered, for 30 minutes until bread crumbs are browned. Remove from oven and let stand 10 minutes before serving.

Magickal Notes

Cheese, glorious cheese! Cheese carries the property of joyful energy. It is also associated with the Moon and the Mother Goddess. It is no wonder we feel such comfort from this old classic of combining it with tender macaroni! The broccoli plays an important role as well in this dish. It brings with it Earth energy and strength. While stirring in the broccoli visualize yourself strong, rooted, and overcoming any hardships in front of you. Coat it in the joyful energy of the cheese. Remember that while this dish is baking in your oven it is a great time to meditate on what hurtles you need to jump and take comfort in the nurturing powers of the Great Mother.

Chapter One: Comfort Foods

Asparagus Soup with Parmesan Sprinkle

Submitted by Tim Titus, Santa Ana, CA

Adapted from *The South Beach Diet Quick & Easy Cookbook,* page 79

I never would have thought of asparagus as a comfort food, but this recipe features one of my favorite spring veggies in a creamy soup, just perfect for a chilly spring evening served with some crispy crackers.

Tim says:

"I am a teacher in Orange County, California, and a student in Christopher Penczak's Witchcraft I Online course. After spending high school eating a steady diet of microwave meals, I resolved to learn to cook and avoid the microwave as an adult. My wife and I have been preparing food together for 13 years. Our kitchen is truly our hearth, the center of our home, where we talk and laugh together while preparing our meals. Although we have only been studying witchcraft for two years, we have been making magick in the kitchen for much longer.

"My wife and I first tried this recipe when we were losing weight. We have made it over and over since then because it is delicious. We make it whenever we can and serve it to everyone when asparagus is in season. It is a great soup for those who love cream soups, but can not eat dairy. The creaminess brings a feeling of warmth, comfort, strength, and vigor, all of which are nice additions to the sensual associations of asparagus."

Ingredients

1 Tablespoon Olive Oil

1 small onion, chopped

1 garlic clove, minced

2 Tablespoons fresh chopped parsley

2 1/2 lbs. asparagus, ends trimmed and cut into 1 1/2 inch
  lengths
4 cups lower-sodium chicken broth
4 teaspoons freshly grated parmesan cheese (optional)
Salt and pepper

Directions

Heat oil over medium heat in a medium saucepan. Add onion, garlic and asparagus and cook, stirring occasionally, until onions soften— 5-7 min. (Do not brown.) Add broth and parsley, bring to a simmer and cook until asparagus is just tender, about 10 minutes. Remove from heat and carefully puree with a blender or hand blender. Return to the pan, gently reheat and season with salt and pepper to taste.

Serve each serving with a sprinkle of parmesan cheese.

Magickal Notes

Asparagus is the key ingredient in this soup. Its magical properties include sexual stamina and male virility. Although usually associated with masculine energy, it may also increase sexual energy in women. This long, phallic shaped vegetable is a wonderful food to eat during the spring and summer months.

Thai Chicken Pasta

Submitted by Tim Titus, Santa Ana CA
Adapted from *Bon Appetit Magazine* in 1999

I love Thai food, an addiction I blame on Christopher Penczak. Our very first lunch was at his favorite Thai restaurant and since I had not tried Thai before I took his recommendation on what to order and the rest is history! Comfort foods, many times, include those *not* homemade dishes like a pint of Chinese takeout or a greasy fast food hamburger. But here, Tim has given us an option to make a spicy, comforting Thai dish right in our own sacred kitchen!

Tim says:

"My wife brought this recipe home from visiting her ailing step-mother, who passed away shortly afterward. We think of her when we serve this dish. After we try a dish the first time, we usually write notes on our impressions and any changes we would make. The recipe card is very dirty from constant use, and the notation simply reads, "So good!" It has become one of our all-time favorite dishes, almost our signature dish. Traditionally, we enjoy it on the night before the first day of school. This dish is excellent cold and could be brought to pot lucks as a cold salad or eaten in individual portions as a cold leftover, great for lunch the next day."

Ingredients

Marinade:

1/4 cup olive oil

1 teaspoon sesame oil

3 Tablespoons soy sauce

1/3 cup rice vinegar

1 bunch green onions, chopped

1 jalapeno pepper, chopped fine

4 cloves garlic, minced

1/4 cup fresh basil (or sweet basil) chopped

2 teaspoons lime juice

2 teaspoons chili garlic sauce

1/4 teaspoon Tabasco sauce

1/4 teaspoon pepper

1/4 teaspoon salt

2 boneless chicken breasts cut in chunks

1 lb. linguine pasta (or rice noodles) cooked al dente

3/4 lb. frozen broccoli florets

1/2 cup cashew nuts, crushed (optional)

Directions

Begin the pasta boiling. Combine all marinade ingredients in a small bowl. Spray a large nonstick pan with cooking spray and, sauté the chicken with approximately 3 Tablespoons of the marinade. Cook 7-10 minutes, until chicken no longer pink. Strain pasta, add broccoli, marinade, and chicken. Mix together and serve topped with crushed cashews.

Hugo's Sloppy Joes

Submitted and created by Leslie Hugo, Sandy, UT

What could bring us back to warm laughter filled nights like our favorite meal from childhood? When we share those food memories with our loved ones we just keep the circle of love and joy flowing. This recipe takes me back to when life was simpler and dinner was always a family occasion.

Leslie says:

"I was raised in the Chicago suburbs, in a home where meals were cooked from scratch. I still have many old recipes handed down, hand-written on old yellowed paper that I cannot part with. I still prefer to cook meals from scratch, using fresh organic ingredients whenever possible."

"This recipe has been handed down from my grandmother, to my mother, to me. It was one of my favorite meals my mom made for me as a child. Mom would make it and all my friends would come over for lunch. We would also make it for family reunions and picnics"

Ingredients

2 pounds ground beef (turkey or tofu can be substituted)
1 large onion, diced
2 1/4 cups catsup
1 cup canned tomato sauce
1 teaspoon mustard
4 Tablespoons brown sugar
4 Tablespoons Worcestershire sauce
1 package buns

Directions

In a large skillet, brown meat and drain excess fat. In large pot, mix the catsup, tomato sauce, mustard and Worcestershire sauce. Stir in the brown sugar. Add the meat to the sauce. Heat on low for half an hour. Serve on buns.

Magickal Notes

Tomatoes are a Love food, so this recipe is definitely a love recipe. Not the romantic love you might think, but love for family and that special love shared from mother to daughter when recipes like this one are handed down. When making this recipe remember to focus on the love that binds all who will share it. And focus on keeping them safe with the onions. These are good for protection both on the spiritual and physical levels because they banish negativity.

Old World Italian Meatballs and Gravy

Submitted and created by Richard Ravenhawke, Gatineau, Quebec, Canada

Anyone who has ever enjoyed a Sunday dinner with
someone Italian knows meatballs and gravy is a staple in
our homes! Most people would say, "Isn't it called Sauce?"
Well, yes and no. Gravy denotes meatballs actually
cooked *in* it where as a sauce is generally put on top.
Richard provides a new take on this classic Italian
comfort food.

Richard says:

"This is my own recipe created from years of hanging out
with older generations in Italian kitchens and learning from the
true master chefs: The family Matriarchs Mamas and Nonas
alike.

"Meatballs are a staple of any traditional Southern Italian
family. Being half Southern Italian I have been privy to many
amazing dishes that include the addition of the meatball. There
is nothing more impressive in my opinion as a nice big plate of
meatballs dripping with sauce sitting in the middle of the
dinner table. I make this recipe often as a comfort food for
grounding and to bring back childhood memories that
stimulate inner child consciousness and a sense of personal
peace. I make it often when entertaining company and new
guests. It is a 'feel good' food everyone loves and always asks for
seconds. The effect of this recipe when made with magickal
intention of bringing together friends is always inner comfort
and peace.

"I have built my career around being a successful psychic
reader and spiritual guide. I have been featured on television
over 500 times and the radio over 300 and my accomplishments
include having my own National psychic radio network for

three years and a global clientele in Politics.
www.ravenhawkpsychic.com

"My Magickal background is eclectic and comes from several schools. I try to put aside religious dogma and attack magick at its core, breaking everything down to the 3 laws, 4 principals and 1 concept of magick that remains Universal through all schools. As a result, my students benefit from a deepened understanding of the common denominators that tie all schools together. It is only through strong roots that any tree can grow to its fullest potential.

Food and recipes are things I have started exploring and I am having a lot of fun learning new things and sharing information with other Fraters and Sorors on the Magickal path to wisdom and enlightenment."

Meatballs Ingredients

1 lb. each of ground beef, ground veal, and ground pork (3 lbs. meat total)

1 whole medium Spanish onion, chopped fine

1/2 cup of grated parmesan cheese

1 16 oz. container of bread crumbs

2 whole eggs

1 whole bulb of garlic

1/4 cup chopped Italian parsley

1/4 quarter cup chopped fresh basil

1 Tablespoon salt

2 Tablespoons black pepper

1 cup water

Gravy Ingredients

6 red tomatoes, cut into pieces

1 whole yellow pepper, chopped

Half of an orange pepper, chopped
Half of a large Spanish onion, chopped fine
1 teaspoon salt
1 Tablespoon finely chopped basil
1 cube chicken bouillon

Directions for Gravy

In a blender, combine tomatoes, peppers, onion, salt, and basil. Blend on high speed until mixed thoroughly. Set aside while you make the meatballs.

Directions for Meatballs

In a large container mix together the three meats with 1 cup of water; mix thoroughly.

Dice and mix in onion and garlic, which has been finely chopped.

Add two whole eggs and kneed into mixture. Mix in the rest of the ingredients, saving the parmesan and bread crumbs until last. If mixture seems too wet, add more bread crumbs slowly to compensate. Form mixture into 1.5 - 3 inch diameter meatballs according to taste and personal preference. (Traditional Italian meatballs are always cooked right in the sauce to produce a gravy.)

Cooking the Meatballs

In a large skillet or sauce pan, heat up 1/2 cup of sauce mixture and add the chicken bouillon cube, make sure it is mixed in well. Add meatballs 6 at a time. Cook on medium heat, occasionally and carefully turning over the meatballs for 20-25 minutes. Add more sauce as needed to the pan as it evaporates and gets absorbed through cooking.

Once the meatballs are cooked, remove them and make room for the next batch and repeat.

This recipe should make approx. 12 - 15 large meatballs. Serve 1 – 2 meatballs per person with bread and pasta, vegetable or any other side dish of choice.

Magickal Notes

Meat is kinship and prosperity food. That might be why we Italians tend to make meatballs when we want to show love or share friendship with neighbors and family. Although there are tomatoes in this recipe for love, peppers for fire energy, and onions for protection from evil I want to focus on the meat. Meat (beef in particular) was always a sign of wealth and prosperity in ancient days. Only the wealthy feasted on meat where the poor had bread. So share these meatballs with friends and family and welcome prosperity and friendship into your kitchen.

Cheesy Zippy Rice Casserole

Submitted by Kristine Dice, Missouri City, Texas

A cheesy bubbling casserole right from the oven warms your heart and your home on a cold winter's night. Seems that lots of comfort foods come right from the oven to eager bellies and smiling faces. Here is a quick and easy casserole you can make just as is for a great side dish or "beef" it up with some leftover chicken or ham, or fancy it up with some veggies for a full dinner!

Kristine says:

"Having been a working mother, working with other women in the same situation, exchanging one-dish recipes was commonplace. This is just one of many such dishes that are quick, easy to fix, and attractive to children and husbands. It was passed around among a group with whom we used to socialize about 35 years ago.

"This dish can be prepared in very little time, and I have served it with everything from gumbo to steaks. Once the rice is cooked, the prep time is only about 20 minutes. All of our three grown children love this dish, and usually ask me to fix it on their birthdays. One likes it with jalapeno peppers and green onions, another likes it with broccoli, and the third likes asparagus and cubed ham. The dish is very versatile. It can be made with just about anything that goes with Monterrey Jack cheese and rice. It's one of those dishes that travels well and goes with any sort of food just by changing the vegetable content. By the way, it's even better reheated the next day!"

Ingredients

4 cups of cooked Rice (white or Brown)
12 ounces of shredded Monterrey Jack Cheese
1/4 to 1/2 cup of minced Jalapeno Peppers
1/2 to 1 cup of Green Onions, about 1/4 inch slices, to taste
12 ounces Sour Cream
1/2 to 1 stick of Butter (to taste)
Salt and Pepper to taste
*Add-in options: one cup Broccoli florets, cubed cooked
  ham, chicken, or turkey.

Directions

Preheat oven to 350 degrees. Put the cooked rice into a large bowl, mix in the sour cream, about 8 ounces of the cheese, most of the butter (cut into pats), the Green Onions and Jalapeno Peppers, and Salt and Pepper. (Stir in any add-ins you are using at this time as well.) Spray a large oven safe casserole dish with cooking spray. Spread mixture evenly in casserole dish. Top with remaining cheese and butter. Bake for 20–30 minutes until cheese on top is bubbling.

Magickal Notes

It is right there in the name of this recipe: *cheesy*! This ooey gooey casserole is filled with cheese and cream and butter. The cream and butter are associated with the powers of the moon, linked with nurturing energy familiar in so many comfort foods. But the real power here is in the cheese: Powered by Saturn, cheeses help us to persist through hard times. With this rich and bubbling casserole nurture the power of perseverance and enjoy!

Chapter 2:
Heirloom Magick

"After a good dinner, one can forgive anybody,

even one's own relatives."

– Oscar Wilde

Heirloom Magick is instrumental the world of the Kitchen Witch. What do I mean by this? Well, what I like to call Heirloom Magick you might just think of as Grandma's pudding recipe, or Uncle Jimbo's Jambalaya. It is in our blood, our very genetics. It is the process by which we have learned to cook, and learned to love to cook.

Seems I am a Kitchen Witch from a long line of Kitchen Witches, as so many of us are. Mine just happen to be Italian Catholic and would never ever admit to being Witches or Strega! Cooking, baking, and sharing those things with the people I love is not just something I do but it is what I grew up doing. I learned from a young age that Sunday dinners were for family time. So many of us just figure this is something our moms made us do so we would all sit in one place for an hour without interruption. But when you really think about it, these family meals are where learning and sharing really happen the most.

The idea of Heirloom Kitchen Magick, to me, is the food traditions we share through the years. It is funny to think that Mom's pot roast can hold that much magick, because it was never one of your favorites. But think, for a moment, why she made it the way she did. Did she smother it in onions? Did she do that because it was the way her mom used to do it? So much of our family history is handed down through stories and through food. If you really want to learn about your family and where you come from, take a look at the food in the region your ancestors came from. It is interesting to see how some of those foods have found their ways into our own hearts and kitchens.

When my grandmother passed away this past May for the first time I realized how much of what I do, and how I do it, is because of her. Not just the genetic link between human beings, but the likes and dislikes of things. She had a real sweet tooth and loved anything crunchy. She would keep her bread in the toaster until just before it was burned and then scoop jams and marmalades onto it to accompany a steaming cup of coffee. It was not until she passed away that I realized I do the same thing!

When she passed to the Summerland my mother asked me what I would like from Grandma's home. My response was "*anything* from the kitchen!" To my delight my mom soon presented me with a box full of Grandma's old baking tins and roasting pans. My favorites are the muffin tins. They are hammered tin. They came over when my great-grandparents brought my grandma and her brothers and sisters to America almost a century ago. They have been in the family since Italy. The power and the magick they hold is old and wise. Things just seem to taste better when cooked in them.

Heirloom Kitchen Magick is all about staying connected to our ancestors through food and cooking. We invite them to join us in the kitchen as we create our own traditions by tweaking their recipes. They join us in our homes when we celebrate their memory and how much they have shaped our lives. And we go forward teaching our children our secret family recipes so that one day they will share these dishes with those they love!

Pasta Fagioli

This recipe is so very simple. To be honest, I am not sure how far back in my family it goes. I know it is a favorite of my Dad's. My Mother starts to make it in the early Fall months. Its garlic and tomato aroma mixes with the Autumn air and fresh baked bread in my parents' house. But I don't know if this recipe started with my mother or my grandmother. For all I know she could have gotten it out of housekeeping magazine. I guess I will never know! This recipe is also featured in my cookbook *Cucina Aurora Cook Book, a Collection of Recipes for the Novice Kitchen Witch,* but I really wanted to share it here!

Ingredients

4 cloves garlic, chopped

2 Tablespoons olive oil

2 8 oz. cans tomato sauce

2 cups water

2 cans cannelloni beans (white kidney beans), drained

1 Tablespoon oregano

1 teaspoon ground black pepper

Pinch salt

1/2 box ditalini or elbow pasta

Grated Romano cheese for topping

Directions

In a large skillet heat oil on medium heat and cook garlic until soft and just browned. Add tomato sauce and water. Add beans, oregano, salt, and pepper. Simmer on medium low heat 20-30 minutes or until sauce reduces and thickens. Meanwhile, cook pasta to package instructions. Drain and add to bean mixture just before serving. Spoon into large bowls and top with grated cheese. Serve hot with warm bread.

Magickal Notes

Beans are a food synonymous with divination and decision making. Although this meal is fast and perfect for a crisp Fall night, make it when wrestling with a difficult or important decision. While stirring, trace the Pentacle in the sauce. Focus on the choices in front of you. Invite your ancestors to come and guide you through the process of decision making. Share with them your hopes and fears. Allow them to advise you in your dreams, visions or meditations after eating this meal.

Chapter Two: Heirloom Magick

Roasted Red Pepper Salad

I cannot remember a birthday, holiday or family dinner that did not involve this simple dish on the table. As a child I would always try it and never liked it. I would see all the grown-ups gobbling it up and could not understand what the big deal was! Now I know. This dish is especially wonderful in the summer months when peppers and tomatoes are at their peak.

Ingredients

3 red peppers
3 large tomatoes
3 cloves garlic, chopped
1 Tablespoon olive oil, plus 2 more for dressing the salad
1 Tablespoon fresh parsley, chopped
Pinch crushed hot red pepper
Salt and pepper to taste

Directions

Turn the oven broiler on High. Coat each pepper with olive oil and place on cookie sheet or shallow baking pan. Place peppers closest to the top of the oven. Broil about 3 minutes until black spots start to form on peppers. Using tongs or a fork, carefully turn peppers over. Peppers will be VERY hot. Return to heat. Broil another 3 minutes until skins begin to get dark. Remove from oven and place them in a large bowl. Cover with plastic wrap sealed tight so no air can get through. Let stand 20 minutes. Meanwhile, cut up tomatoes into bite side pieces. Put them in a medium bowl with garlic, parsley, crushed red pepper, salt and pepper. Once roasted peppers are cool, remove the stems and gently peel off the skin. Cut the peppers into large bite size pieces, being sure to remove any ribs, membrane or seeds that remain in the pepper. Add roasted peppers to tomato mixture. Serve cool by itself, with soft seeded Italian bread, or over chicken

Magickal Notes

It is no surprise that with Pepper comes the power of Fire and the Sun God. Paired here with a love food like tomatoes, the peppers bring heat back into relationships. That said, this power is not exclusively for romantic relationships. If a friendship has gone cool, or you want to bring warmth to a loved one who seems to need it share this dish with them. This dish is also wonderful for any event that celebrates masculine energy; Father's Day for example. If you would like to mellow out the Fire Energy, pair this with some fresh mozzarella cheese to bring in mothering and nurturing energy.

Classic Sugar Cookie Cutouts

I debated with myself over and over about this recipe. Should I put it in the book, and where it should go? When I thought on it and took a moment to step back, what I realized was so many of my earliest memories in the kitchen were of baking cookies for the Christmas season with my Mother. It is a little odd to mention Christmas baking in a Pagan cookbook, but so many of us still hold on to those Holiday traditions we were brought up with. And so many of those are centered around food. So here is this recipe in the Heirloom section of the book because I know it is one I will hand down in years to come.

Ingredients

Cookies

3 1/4 cups flour

1/2 teaspoon salt

1 Tablespoon baking powder

1 cup sugar

1 1/2 sticks butter, softened

2 eggs

1 Tablespoon Vanilla

Frosting

1 egg white

1/8 teaspoon cream of tartar

1/8 teaspoon vanilla

1 3/4 cups confectioner's sugar

Directions

In a medium bowl, combine flour baking soda, and salt. Set aside. In a large bowl beat, on medium speed, butter and sugar until light and fluffy. Beat in eggs and vanilla. Slowly mix in flour mixture in 1/4 cup increments, blending well to make a stiff dough. Form into a ball and wrap in plastic wrap. Chill at least one hour or overnight.

Preheat oven to 350 degrees. Line cookie sheets with parchment paper. Roll out dough on lightly floured surface. Cut out with your choice of cookie cutters: Trees, Goddesses, Reindeer, etc. place cut out shapes on prepared cookie sheets and bake for 10 minutes or until lightly browned. Remove to wire racks and cool completely before decorating with frosting, sprinkles, and candy.

Frosting: Mix all frosting ingredients together and fill a pastry bag with your desired pastry tip with frosting. Ice cookies as you desire! If you would like to have different colored frosting, use food coloring and mix into frosting when you make it.

Magickal Notes

This recipe is so very simple and wonderful and although there are magickal properties in these ingredients the real power here comes from whatever shape you choose to make your cookies in. Try using Christmas tree shaped cutters to symbolize the Yule tree, or Star shapes for the power of the Pentacle. A Goddess cookie cutter celebrates the Great Mother and can be used for all occasions. It is important to note that these can be made in the shape of butterflies for Beltane Celebrations or Rabbits for Ostara. Use your imagination when picking shapes and you will have new traditions for every Sabbat!

Spaghetti Pie

I am sure there is a big fancy Italian word for this dish, but I don't know it. In our house, like so many others it was simply known as Spaghetti Pie. My husband and I were chatting about our favorite family recipes that we grew up on and we both remembered this dish. Both of our mothers used to make this with leftover spaghetti. It always felt like a special treat. Every time this pie was made it was a little bit different; sometimes there would be no tomato sauce on the leftover pasta and sometimes there would be a ton, sometimes it would be covered in melty mozzarella cheese and sometimes topped with toasted breadcrumbs, but every time was delicious.

Ingredients

1-2 cups leftover spaghetti (or freshly cooked)

3 cloves garlic, chopped

1/2 large sweet onion, chopped

2 Tablespoons olive oil

6 eggs

1/4 cup fresh parsley

1/2 cup ricotta cheese

1 Tablespoon grated Parmesan cheese

pinch dried basil

salt and pepper to taste

Directions

Heat oven to 350 degrees. Spray a large pie plate with cooking spray and set aside. In a large bowl, whisk eggs until light and fluffy. Whisk in parsley, ricotta, parmesan, basil, salt, and pepper. Set aside. In a large skillet, heat olive oil. Sauté garlic and onions until just tender, about 5 minutes. Turn off heat and add spaghetti. Toss to coat in oil mixture. Place spaghetti mixture into prepared pie plate and pour egg mixture over it. Carefully place in oven and bake for 30 minutes or until eggs are set. Serve hot or cold, for breakfast, lunch or dinner with a side salad or fruit.

Magickal Notes

In my home it is true magick to get a second full meal out of seemingly unrelated leftover items in the fridge. My mother has been doing that for years! This recipe has been changed and handed down for years to each generation and each family makes it a little different. Eggs are always known for their fertility powers, and here in this recipe, they are a symbol of the fertility of the family and its traditions. Make this dish with the intention of watching your family grow in size, health, and prosperity. You can also make this dish to encourage growth and fertility for others as well.

Albanian Spinach Pie

Submitted by Bob Pando, Watertown, MA

I love Greek spinach pie. Since my husband doesn't care for feta cheese, which is traditionally used in the dish, this Albanian version is just the right amount of creamy cheese and spinach between flakey and golden phyllo dough. Bob keeps it really simple by using frozen phyllo, which you can find in the freezer section of just about any grocery store.

Bob says:

"I'm not a witch, although my wife and her friends claim I work magic in my small city garden. I get the greatest pleasure from growing my own plants from seed – mostly tomatoes, culinary herbs, blueberries, even cherries. My Albanian family is filled with talented cooks, my mother especially. I learned to cook by watching her and enjoy preparing traditional recipes and experimenting with new ones when the mood strikes.

"This recipe was adapted by me from one handed down through the generations in my family. It is similar to the Greek spanakopita; however, I think the Albanian version is older and much better. It has been simplified by using prepared phyllo dough for the crust. This is one of our holiday favorites. When made for New Year's, a coin is placed in the pie. It is said that the recipient of the coin will have good luck and prosperity for the New Year."

Ingredients

Crust
1 box frozen Phyllo dough
1 lb. butter, melted

Filling
1 lb. whole milk cottage cheese

8 oz. shredded Monterey jack cheese

8 oz. shredded cheddar cheese

8 eggs

4 16 oz. bags fresh spinach

1 Tablespoon olive oil

Directions

Clean spinach by removing stem ends and spines. In a large sauce pan heat oil and add spinach. Let spinach wilt but do not cook too long. Be sure *not* to brown! Add cottage cheese, shredded cheeses, and mix well. Add eggs and mix thoroughly. Remove from heat and set aside.

Preheat oven to 350 degrees. Brush bottom of a cookie sheet with melted butter and place a single layer of dough on top; brush dough completely with butter and top with another single layer of dough. Repeat these steps until you have six buttered layers of dough in the pan. Pour filling and spread evenly over dough. Prepare the top crust of the pie the same way as you did the bottom: a layer of dough, brushed with butter and so forth until you have six buttered layers on top. Trim edges of crust as needed to fit pan. Bake for 20-30 minutes, until golden brown and flaky. Remove from oven and let sit for 10-15 minutes before cutting. Serve warm or refrigerate and serve as a cold dish.

Magickal Notes

I found it really interesting that Bob makes a point to tell us that during the holidays whoever finds the coin in this pie will have a prosperous year. Spinach is a money food. Actually, most leafy greens can be used magically to protect, grow, and attract money and physical wealth. This is a prosperity dish in all ways! When you add the eggs, which are just full of fertility power, to the spinach, focus on your investments growing.

Sweet & Spicy Baked Apples

Submitted by Edain McCoy
Recipe Created by Mary A. Sharp Modlin

Edain says:

"Apples are plentiful in central and southern Indiana. This was once Johnny Appleseed's planting grounds. My great-grandmother is credited for this recipe, though it is likely it was one shared by many farm women of Delaware County, each putting her own unique fingerprint on the basic recipe. My mother was given this recipe from her mother-in-law (Mary's youngest child) and has made many pans full of these sweet and spicy dishes ever since.

"I have been a Witch since 1981. Since then I have studied followed made-in-the-Americas traditions, learning something new and exciting with each. I am a historian, graduate student, a speaker at Pagan festivals, and the author of over twenty books on Witchcraft, magick, and the occult arts. Find me on Facebook or my website, *www.EdainMcCoy.com*"

Ingredients

Apples to fit a 13 x 9 Pyrex pan (about 6–8 depending on size)

1 cup sifted flour

1 cup granulated sugar

1 cup corn syrup

2/3 cup cold water

Cinnamon to taste

Allspice and/or nutmeg (optional to taste)

Red food coloring (optional)

Directions

Peal the apples then halve or quarter them into the Pyrex pan, disposing of core and seeds. Mix in all other ingredients thoroughly, adding spices to taste. Red food coloring gives the dish a festive look, but is optional. Bake at 350 until apples are tender, 25-40 minutes depending on depth of pan and your oven's calibration. Use a fork to test for tenderness level.

Magickal Notes

Apples are a truly magical food with much mythology surrounding them. Yes, apples are for love and health, but when we cook them down like in this recipe they help bring peace and comfort to our hearts and spirits. Edain also had some wonderful magical information about this dish:

"For the Celts, the land of apples, or Avalon, stood between the world of the living and the dead. Apples cut crosswise show the inner-pentagram and, though the fruit is healthy and robust, the seeds inside contain deadly cyanide. Apples are used in passing over rites, for spells for mental pursuits, love, beauty, connection to the otherworld, and as gifts for the dead and for the guardian spirits of cemeteries."

Cacoila (Portuguese Pulled Pork)

Submitted by Rich Dupere, Bristol RI

Food can link us to our family history. If you want to know
the culture of a people, look at what they eat. We can learn
what is abundant in that part of the world and understand why
our family members still love it today. Different cultures can
take the same main ingredient and make completely different
meals from it because of the different spices or herbs native to
that part of the world. It is amazing how these recipes survive
time and distance. Rich shares with us one of his favorite
recipes handed down from Portugal.

Rich says:

"I am a dedicate of Hecate who works heavily with energy
work and magick. I work with everything from Reiki and
spiritual guidance to cooking and food magick. Creativity and
healing are heavily immersed in my practice, especially in the
kitchen.

"This recipe came from the old country of Portugal. After
begging and bribing my aunt, who had my Vavo's (Portuguese
Grandmother) recipe for two solid years she finally sent it to
me. I love this recipe for its spiciness and kick. For anyone who
wants a taste of the old country, this one's for you. From juicy
pork to the explosion of spices on your taste buds, this recipe
will not leave you wanting. Well, maybe for a glass of water.
Potatoes are often used. Basting them in the broth is a great
idea to add to this dish. I hope you are hungry!"

Ingredients

4 lbs. blade meat pork
1 Tablespoon salt
2 Tablespoons hot crushed red pepper
2 Tablespoons pickling spice

1/4 cup red wine vinegar

2 Tablespoons allspice

4 Bay leaves, crushed

2 cloves of garlic, whole

2 large potatoes cut into large chunks (optional)

Directions

Put the allspice, bay leaves, and garlic into a piece of cheesecloth and tie together, making a small bag. Place the meat in a large roasting pan and fill with water to just below the top of the meat. Add the vinegar, salt, and crushed pepper. Put the bag of spices in the pan with the water and put in the refrigerator to marinate overnight. Preheat oven to 350 degrees. Put the pan in the oven and cook for about 2 hours basting the meat every half hour. At the last half hour, add the potatoes to the liquid and continue cooking until they are tender.

Magickal Notes

Rich calls this a taste of the old country and indeed it is. There are no crock pots or food processors here, just a good old fashion marinade and hearty potatoes. While basting this pork, remember its powers of prosperity. The bay leaf has divination properties. When you are covering the meat in this unique marinate of allspice and bay, try to envision what you want in terms of personal prosperity. Ask the ancestors of the old country to help you learn and grow. Put the intention of drawing sight for future financial goals into this delicious spicy pork dish. Use the grounding properties of the potato to help stay focused on your goals.

Nana's Poultry Stuffing

Submitted by Jocelyn VanBokkelen, South Hampton NH

Most of us have a little old grandma who passed down recipes throughout the years. If yours was anything like mine when you asked "Grandma, can I have that recipe?" she said something like "I don't know, I just make it!" Lots of these handed down recipes call for pinches and dashes and handfuls of things. Somehow we figure them out and are able to recreate these family favorites!

Jocelyn says:

"I spent the first 20 years of my life expecting to be a PhD in the sciences, and the second 20 years being an over-educated organic farmer. Which is to say that I spent the first half of my life avoiding the fact that I was born a witch, and the second half embracing it.

"This recipe was created by my great grandmother, who immigrated to the US in 1914 from Austria. I remember it being the best part of the Thanksgiving dinners of my youth. As far as I know, I am the first person to actually quantify this mixture. In the beginning, Wonder Bread and genuine Kellogg's Rice Krispies were used. I have since made it with homemade white and whole wheat breads and other brands of crispy rice cereal which lend their own particular nuances to this simple stuffing. This quantity will stuff a 6 lb. roasting chicken.

Ingredients

1/3 loaf or 6 thick slices stale bread

1-2 cups hot water

1 small onion, chopped

4 med. cloves fresh garlic (or 1/2 teaspoon garlic powder)

3 Tablespoons butter or chicken fat

2 cups Rice Krispies (or equivalent) cereal

1 egg

1/2 teaspoon poultry seasoning

1/4 teaspoon sage

1/4 teaspoon thyme

Salt and Pepper to taste

Directions

Soak stale bread in hot water to soften and crumble with fingers. Drain. This should be about 2 cups wet bread crumbles. In a large skillet heat butter. Add onions and garlic and cook until onions are translucent but not browned. Lower heat to low and add Rice Krispies and soaked bread; mix together. Add poultry seasoning, sage, thyme, pepper and salt. Mix until combined. Add egg; mix. At this point the stuffing should be quite soggy, if not, add more butter or chicken fat. Continue to fry the stuffing, alternately flattening it in the pan and scraping it off the bottom until it becomes drier, but still sticks together. Seasonings can be adjusted for taste during this frying. Remove from heat and allow to cool somewhat before stuffing bird or serve warm along side turkey or chicken.

Magickal Notes

The main ingredient in this, like so many stuffing's, is the bread. Bread is a kinship and prosperity food. If we share bread, or "break bread" with friends and family we are encouraging prosperous relationships. This traditional stuffing combines energy from the bread with the puffed rice. Rice is another prosperity food. It is no wonder this is a common dish to have at Thanksgiving when we wish to share friendship and be thankful for our blessings with loved ones.

Luchen Kugle (Noodle Pudding)

Submitted by Sandi Liss, Butler, NJ

When we hear the word "pudding" we tend to think of a power in a little box with big red letters that read "J-E-L-L-O". Not so! Puddings have been a staple in so many homes from rice puddings to plum puddings. Kugle is an authentic Jewish dish that is very versatile. Usually made with egg noodles and creamy cheeses, made sweet and served as a dessert or maybe for a morning meal. It makes a wonderful side dish too.

Sandi says:

"This recipe has been adapted over time, but it is basically my grandmother's recipe. She made it without the sugary topping though. Luchen Kugle means Noodle Pudding in Yiddish and is usually a side dish for a main lunch/dinner. This one, however, is an excellent side dish, but also works wonderfully as a dessert. I usually make two pans each year for when the family gets together to celebrate Chanukah. One pan has raisins, the other does not. I still make this dish for friends and am always sending home containers filled with Luchen Kugle with them. Serve it hot or cold, it's just as good either way.

Ingredients

1 lb. egg noodles, cooked to directions on package

1 1/2 sticks butter

1 lb. cream cheese, softened

1/2 pint sour cream

4 eggs

2 teaspoons vanilla

1/4 teaspoons cinnamon (or to taste)

3/4 cup sugar

1/8 teaspoon salt

Topping
1/2 cup sugar
3/4 cup flour
1 stick butter

Directions

Preheat oven to 350 degrees. In large bowl whisk together eggs, vanilla, cinnamon, sugar, and salt and set aside. In medium-sized saucepan melt butter, cream cheese, and sour cream together. Remove from heat and pour into egg mixture. Add cooked noodles and stir until combined. Pour entire mixture into a 9 x 12 pan. Mix together topping ingredients, crumble, and sprinkle over the noodle mixture. Bake for one hour. Serve hot, cut into squares.

Magickal Notes

Dairy foods have a direct association with the Mother Goddess. Milk is the life-sustaining force only a mother can produce for her child. So, it is fitting that in the case of this kugle it has been passed from mother to mother to mother. In this recipe we see milk used in different forms: cream cheese, sour cream, and even the butter have the energy of the Moon. Cook and eat this dish to be closer to the Great Mother but also to experience the Goddess within and identify with the divine feminine. This would be a wonderful dish to make and share for full moon celebrations.

The "Perfect" Crab Cake

Submitted by Gail Wood
Created by the Adkins-Wood Family

Here in New England seafood is one of the most wonderful things you can get your hands on. From clam chowder to lobster rolls, there are restaurants and festivals dedicated to food from the sea at any given time of the year. But Maryland is a place famous for its crab cakes. This simple recipe is so good you will think you are sitting harbor side soaking up the sun!

Ingredients

3 Tablespoons oil
1 lb. cooked crab meat
1 slice bread, crumbled
1 Tablespoon mayonnaise
1 teaspoon mustard
1 egg
Hot pepper flakes, Tabasco to taste
Lemon wedges for serving

Directions

Put all ingredients in a large bowl. Mix well until combined. Shape into cakes. In a large skillet heat oil and fry each cake 3–4 minutes on each side until lightly browned and hot. Serve immediately with fresh lemon wedges.

Magickal Notes

Gail tells us a little about how the Crab lives his life and how we might learn from him. We can apply this information and meditate on it when preparing and eating this dish.

"The crab is a scavenger, a bottom feeder, scurrying to and fro along the shore and in the water. The crab walks sideways, in a circuitous route towards its goal. The crab also has a tough outer shell that protects the soft and vulnerable insides. The wisdom of the crab teaches us discernment about the debris we pick up: are we scavenging for our survival and improvement, or are we picking up debris which does not serve us well? Other lessons of the crab ask us to seek our inner selves and to understand the nature of our hard outer shell. Are we protecting ourselves in order to be all we can be, or is our hard outer shell a shield and a barrier preventing us to find our true heart or our true path?

Crab is the symbol of the sun sign of Cancer, the water sign of home, hearth, family, emotions, and healing. The crab teaches us to use our hearts and our luscious insides to create love, pleasure, home, and welcome."

Baked Eggplant

Submitted by Jean Pando, Watertown, MA

Eggplant is an all time favorite in my Witchy Kitchen. Seems I am not the only one. When late summer comes and the leaves begin to turn color, eggplant is in season. Coming in many different verities from the shiny midnight purple we are all so accustomed to, to the tender white breed. This is a versatile veggie, baked to perfection in this recipe.

Jean says:

"I'm a Temple tradition witch; owing to the fact that while growing up the holidays, especially holiday meals, were always something special, my practice revolves around the seasons, holidays, hearth, and home, always including foods of the season, decorations, and ritual often involving a craft symbolizing the holiday. Coming from an Italian family in which everyone loved to cook—and eat—I found my way around the kitchen at a very young age. Somewhere there are pictures of a three-year-old me flouring smelts to be fried for dinner! One of the things that makes me happiest is preparing a holiday meal to share with family and friends.

"This recipe for Baked Eggplant was handed down to me from my Aunt Josie. It's always been a favorite with family and friends and is an often-requested dish for holidays and special occasions. One of the secrets of this dish is the sauce. Auntie always said that, for the very best flavor, use only this special sauce for the eggplant. Other kinds of sauce may be used, but in my experience, it never tastes as good. Another secret of this dish is peeling, *thinly* slicing, and then salting the eggplant. This is a truly wonderful dish – not your typical eggplant parm! The preparation is like a ritual unto itself and the finished product a true work of kitchen magic. Enjoy!"

Ingredients

Sauce

2 12 oz. cans tomato paste

24 oz. water

3 cloves garlic, minced

1 1/2 Tablespoons dried basil

1 teaspoon oregano

1 teaspoon dried parsley

2 Tablespoons sugar

Black pepper

Salt

1/4 cup olive oil

Black pepper

Salt

1/4 cup olive oil

Eggplant, Breading and Topping

3 medium eggplant

2 or 3 cups bread crumbs

2 Tablespoons basil

2 Tablespoons parsley

2 teaspoons garlic powder

1 Cup grated Romano cheese

3 eggs beaten with a little milk

16 oz. shredded mozzarella cheese

Olive oil

Pinch Salt

Directions

Peel and thinly slice eggplant. Arrange in layers on a large platter or in a colander, sprinkling salt on each layer as you go.

After layering, place another platter (or plate) on top of the eggplant and weigh down with a heavy object or jug of water. Let sit for 30 to 45 minutes to release the moisture and bitterness. Drain the liquid, rinse eggplant and pat dry.

To prepare the sauce, heat the oil in a medium skillet over low heat; add garlic and sauté until soft, about 3 minutes. Add the basil, oregano, parsley, and salt and pepper to taste; simmer for 1 minute. Add tomato paste then add water, stirring thoroughly to make a slightly thick sauce. Simmer covered for 30 minutes, adding a little more water if needed. Add sugar, stir thoroughly and simmer for 10 minutes.

Preheat the oven to 375 degrees. While sauce is simmering, beat eggs and milk together. In a separate bowl, combine bread crumb, parsley, basil, garlic powder, and half of the Romano cheese; mix thoroughly. Dip eggplant in the egg mixture then coat with breading.

Heat oil (about ¼ inch in bottom of pan) in a large skillet over medium high heat. Fry eggplant until golden brown on both sides; place on paper towel-lined plate to absorb excess oil.

Put a thin layer of sauce in the bottom of a 9 x 13 inch baking dish (or two smaller pans); cover with a layer of eggplant; top eggplant with layer of mozzarella cheese and sprinkle some of the remaining Romano. Continue layering in this manner, ending with a final layer of sauce and the cheeses. Bake 45min to an hour until hot and bubbling.

Magickal Notes

Eggplant is one of those versatile vegetables. We associate it mostly with Italian cooking but it originated in China. It can be found in everything from rolittini to stir fry and ratatouille. Eggplant is generally associated with the Earth and if you have ever gotten one fresh from the farmer's market you understand why. They positively hum with the energy of the Earth. Eggplant has Goddess properties due to its woman-like shape.

But remember, Eggplant also helps you hone your spiritual practice. While you are preparing it, focus on the roundness of the vegetable and envision what you would like to accomplish with your spiritual self.

Dad's Easter Pie or "Pizza Chiena"

Submitted by Jean Pando

Easter Pie is something every Italian family I know has a recipe for. And in truth we all think ours is the best. My mom makes it with sliced ham, ricotta cheese and hard boiled eggs but others insist it needs crumbled sausages and onions. Jean Pando gives us another one of her family's recipes and I just had to share it!

Jean says:

"This recipe is my Dad's version of an Italian tradition, "Pizza Chiena" (pronounced "gaina"). It is a crown jewel in my family recipes and a favorite, though not many are willing to admit that they love this decadent dish in this age of lighter fare − I'll admit it's one of my favorites. In my family this pie made an annual appearance during the Easter Holiday. In fact, most Italian bakeries carry it during the Easter season (though none taste as good as this one). Now it has made a quite natural transition to my Ostara celebrations − perfect given the abundance of eggs in the recipe."

Ingredients

Filling
1 lb. Ricotta cheese
3/4 cup grated Romano cheese
1/2 lb. Mozzarella cheese
4 eggs
1 teaspoon black pepper
1/2 lb. piece imported prosciutto
1/4 lb. piece Genoa salami

Pastry
2 cups flour
3 eggs, beaten
1 1/2 teaspoon olive oil
1/2 stick butter
Pinch of salt

Directions

Preheat oven to 375.

Make the filling: Chop meat and mozzarella cheese into very small cubes. Mix together Ricotta and Romano cheeses, eggs, and pepper. Add cubed meat and cheese and mix thoroughly and set aside.

In a large bowl, cream butter until soft and smooth. Gradually fold in oil and beaten eggs until mixed well. Mix baking powder and salt with flour and add gradually to egg mixture until dough is firm but workable. Cut in half, one for bottom one for the top. Roll out each ball of dough to 1/4-inch thickness. Line an 8- or 9-inch round pie plate with one of the crusts. Fill the pie crust with filling. Cover with second pie crust. Pinch together the top and bottom crusts to seal the pie. Bake for 1 hour, or until filling is firm and pick comes out clean. Serve cold or at room temperature.

Magickal Notes

Eggs are a very magickal food. For years people celebrated the Spring holidays of Ostara and Beltane by eating this fertility food. The practice of eating eggs in the spring was adopted from the ancient religions by the Christians for their celebration of Easter. Eggs are not just for feminine fertility, but for fertility in jobs, relationships, and many other things. As you prepare this pie, with each egg you crack and beat, put your intentions for growth of all the things you hope to come into your life through the fertility power of the eggs.

Caputi Spaghetti Sauce

Submitted by Nicole Caputi

Anyone who has ever had spaghetti and meatballs can attest to how the sauce can make or break the meal. That is one reason why I never get anything with a red sauce when I go out to dinner. A real tomato sauce needs to be made with love. Like this one.

Ingredients

3 15 oz. cans of San Marzano tomatoes
2 4 oz. cans of tomato paste
2 large cloves garlic minced
1 large onion chopped
1 Tablespoon oregano
1 Tablespoon basil
1 Tablespoon parsley
1/4 cup grated cheese
small pinch of sugar
Salt & Pepper
2 Tablespoons olive oil
1/2 cup red wine (optional)

Directions

In a large sauce pot, on medium heat, put olive oil, garlic & onion until softened but not browned. Put each can of tomatoes in a blender & mix thoroughly, add to pot. Add spices and grated cheese to taste.

Simmer on low at least 8 hours. Serve warm over pasta.

Magickal Notes

The smell of a big pot of tomato sauce cooking on the stove reminds me of Sunday dinners at my grandmother's house. As I got older it became me who was making this Italian staple for my grandmother and my parents. And of course now I make big batches for my husband and any guests who happen to drop by. Tomato sauce can make anything better; like a kiss on your knee when you fell off your bike as a child. These little red fruits were once thought to be poison but really hold so much love energy. Tomato not only helps us to attract love into our lives, but it also helps us to accept love. Better still, tomatoes help us to *give* love. When making this recipe you want to stir it about every hour or so. At that time write, with your wooden spoon, the names of those you will be sharing this sauce with. And be sure to draw hearts and pentacles in the sauce as well to protect your loved ones.

Traditional Hungarian Fare

Submitted by Ayrzabet.

So much of our family and cultural traditions are passed down through stories and food. Who ate these dishes in generations past and at what celebrations? When we learn about what our own ancestors ate and how they lived we learn so much about ourselves. The next few recipes are traditional Hungarian dishes passed down through the years!

Hungarian Poppy Seed Moon Cake (*Makosbeigli*)

Ayrzabet says:

"This is a recipe handed down by the women in the family, one generation to the next. It is believed the recipe is of Romani (gypsy) origin. Poppy seeds were associated with the moon in ancient times in Eastern Europe and offered to the moon during pagan celebration. The seeds are still called 'Moon seeds' in German. The Poppy seeds should be finely ground for the recipe. You can grind your own seeds in a coffee grinder. Grind the seeds well as it will make a big difference in the texture.

"These cakes can be wrapped in foil and stored in the freezer after they are baked."

Ingredients

Dough

4 cups flour

4 Tablespoons sugar

1 cup lukewarm water

2 eggs, slightly beaten

2 cakes yeast, regular or dry

1/2 cup soft butter

1 teaspoon salt

Filling
1 pound finely ground poppy seeds
2 cups sugar
1 cup boiled milk
1/4 cup melted butter
2 teaspoons grated lemon zest

Directions

Preheat oven to 350. Spray two baking sheets with cooking spray.

Make the filling: combine poppy seeds, sugar, ¾ cup of milk, butter and lemon zest. It should be thick. If not spreadable use the rest of milk. Divide the mixture into 4 portions, one for each dough rollup.

Make the dough: Crumble yeast in bowl, add water and sugar stirring till mixture completely dissolves. Blend flour and butter with wire pastry blender. Mix well, mix in eggs, salt and yeast. Mix until dough is smooth and leaves side of bowl clean. *Do not let rise!* Divide into four sections and roll each out in a rectangular shape spread with filling and roll up like Jelly Roll. Place on baking pans. Bake for 30 to 45 minutes or until brown.

Makes 4 cakes.

Magickal Notes

The poppy seeds connect us with the divine feminine in these not too sweet cakes. These would be a great addition to any celebration where women's mysteries are being celebrated. Make them while feeling grounded and rooted in your female energy.

Hungarian Stuffed Cabbage (*Toltottkaposzta*)

Ayrzabet says:

"It is an old custom among Hungarians to eat cooked cabbage on New Year's day. It is believed that by doing so, you will have money in the new year to support you and your family. Cabbage is associated with the Goddess Fortuna and the Goddess Hekate."

Ingredients

2 pounds of ground beef

2 teaspoon salt

1 Tablespoon Hungarian paprika

1/2 teaspoon ground pepper

1 cup of instant white or brown rice

15 oz. can tomato sauce

1 large white onion chopped (divide into 2 portions)

1 large head of cabbage

2 family size cans condensed tomato soup

4 regular size cans condensed cream of celery soup

1 Tablespoon lemon juice

1/2 cup water

Directions

Preheat oven to 375. In a large mixing bowl, add ground beef, 1/2 of the onion, tomato sauce, salt, paprika, pepper and rice. Mix well with clean hands. Set aside.

Take out the core of the cabbage. Leave head whole. Place in large pot of boiling water to wilt the outer leaves. You will be able to gently pull off whole cabbage leaves. Trim off thick center vein of cabbage leaves. Make a pile of leaves on your work station. You may want to shake excess water off. When you get to the point where the leaves are too small or too difficult to pull apart chop the rest of the cabbage and set aside. Place two Tablespoons of meat and rice mixture on a leaf (starting at the thick end) and roll it up and tuck in ends with your finger. Make as many as you can. Arrange the rolls in a large roasting pan. If you have remaining meat and rice mixture, roll into large balls and place on top of the cabbage rolls. Layer chopped cabbage and remaining onion over the top of the cabbage rolls.

In another large bowl, combine with whisk the tomato, celery soup, lemon juice and water. Pour over the top of the rolls, making sure all are covered.

Bake, covered for one hour, making sure the meat filling is cooked. Serve warm with crusty bread.

Magickal Notes

Cabbage is a leafy green and therefore associated with money, wealth and prosperity. It is no wonder that Hungarian tradition notes that eating this dish at the New Year will bring monetary gain in the coming year! What is also of note here is that the ground beef is a kinship food associated with wealth and the rice has prosperity energy. Make this dish with mindfulness, envisioning you, your family and your friends surrounded in comfortable wealth!

Hungarian Plum Dumplings (*Szilvas gomboc*)

Ayrzabet says:

"Plum (both fruit and juice) is an appropriate food for love spells. Plums are associated with Aphrodite, Hekate, and Isis. Plum dumplings are a treat many people have never had. Plump potato dough surrounding a pitted plum juicy with sugar and cinnamon, and swimming in buttered bread crumbs. When you cut into them the purple juices run out like a garnet river. Plum dumplings are eaten alone as a meal."

Ingredients

30 Free Stone Italian plums, washed, split, pitted

4 or 5 medium sized Potatoes, peeled

1 egg, beaten

4 cups flour

1 teaspoon salt

Buttered bread crumbs

Sugar

Cinnamon

Directions

Fill a large pot 3/4 full with water. Add a pinch of salt. Cook potatoes in salted water till soft. Drain and mash the potatoes and add warm to flour and salt on a kneading surface. Make a well and add egg and knead gently till all is blended. On a clean floured surface, roll dough out to 1/2 inch thick. Cut dough into 4 inch squares and put a plum into the center of each square. Place 1/2 teaspoon sugar and a sprinkle of cinnamon in the hole of the plum. Fold corners to the middle and roll the dumpling in your hands till round. Set aside. Bring another pot of salted water to boil. Cook a few dumplings at a time in salted water for about 10 minutes. Remove with a slotted spoon.

Place in a baking pan in which bread crumbs have been toasted in butter (one cup crumbs to 1/4 cup butter) and mixed with 1/2 cup of sugar and 2 teaspoons cinnamon. Keep warm.

When all the dumplings have been cooked and are in the baking pan, gently spoon the bread crumbs, butter, sugar and cinnamon mix over all.

Serve warm with bread crumb topping.

Magickal Notes

Plums are indeed a food of many goddesses. They hold feminine lustful powers. These little juicy fruits are used to heighten the capacity for arousal in both men and women. Eating these little plum dumplings not only brings the unexpected to the dinner table but also to the bedroom! Be open to sharing these with your spouse or lover. Prepare them together with visualization of a night to remember.

Chapter 3:
Pantry Magick

"Cooking is like love; it should be entered into
with abandon or not at all."

− Harriet Von Horne

On occasion, when I teach a class on Kitchen Witchery, there will be someone in the group who claims they are a terrible cook. The first thing I tell them is if one thinks they are a terrible cook, then they are right. And if you believe you are a good cook, you are also right. The second thing I tell them is you don't have to be a world class master chef to implement Kitchen Magick into your every day routine. Many of the most magickal dishes are made with what I like to call, "pantry magick."

Pantry magick, as I define it, is using those things you have laying about your cupboards and cabinets to make something truly wonderful. Think about simple, fun recipes that come from condensed soup cans and crushed up corn flake cereals. These are the quick dinners and no-bake desserts children ask for and you make on a regular basis. I categorize things like green bean casserole in this section of food magick. Think about it, mushroom soup, fried onions, and frozen string beans. What could be simpler?

Instant foods also fit into this category. There is no need to fire up all four burners on your stove and chop for hours to make something spectacular. And let's be honest, we don't live in a world where that is possible on an everyday basis. Some mornings we are just lucky enough to shove a slice of toast and peanut butter down our throats as we sit in traffic on the way to the office. This is real life and, unfortunately, this is how we eat sometimes. But when we make that toast with intention, and remember that peanut butter is a prosperity food, it can become full of spiritual nutrition to help us handle the day ahead of us.

Things like pancake and brownie mixes line our cupboards for quick, easy treats we can whip up at a moment's notice in case company comes calling. Because these items come from a box does that make them less magickal? The answer is no. Although I prefer to do things from scratch, and cooking with the freshest ingredients helps us stay closer to Mother Earth, these supermarket staples are part our lives and our culture. I recommend you try to stock your cabinets with healthier options, like whole wheat pancake mix and all natural cake mixes and try to stay away from canned goods high in MSG or Nitrates. But remember intentional cooking is the key to Kitchen Magick. Even if you are microwaving a TV dinner, do it with a joyful, loving heart!

Crunchy Chicken Fingers with Honey Mustard

On rainy nights I tend to crave some junk food. Like most of us I have the guilt that comes along with wanting this type of food. It is good to indulge in things like hot dogs, and French fries from time to time. One thing I just *love* is chicken figures. This recipe is an easy quick and healthier version of what we are used to getting at restaurants and fast food joints. I like to gobble these up with a side of baked tatter tots or sweet potato fries.

Ingredients

1 lb. chicken tenderloins

1 large egg

1/4 cup milk

1 cup corn flakes cereal, crushed

1/2 cup corn meal

1/4 cup bread crumbs

1 teaspoon granulated onion

Pinch salt

Pinch paprika

4 Tablespoons olive oil

Directions

In a large bowl combine crushed corn flakes, corn meal, bread crumbs, granulated onion, salt, and paprika. Set aside. In a shallow bowl, beat egg and milk until combined and slightly fluffy. In a large skillet, heat olive oil. Dredge chicken tenderloins one by one in the egg wash mixture and then in the corn flake mixture. Be sure the chicken is coated on all sides with cornflake mixture. Place lightly in the heated oil. Cook about 3-4 minutes on each side or until chicken is cooked through and the crust is slightly golden brown and crunchy.

Drain on paper towel. Serve warm with honey mustard for dipping.

Honey mustard dipping sauce: Combine ¼ cup mayonnaise, 2 Tablespoons of brown mustard and 1 Tablespoon of honey in a small bowl, stir until combined.

Magickal Notes

Chicken is a health and wellness food. Although when we see traditional chicken fingers they do not generally aid our health and well being! In this case they are lightly fried in olive oil and covered in corn flakes. Corn is a food that represents the cycles of the seasons. As you fry these crispy little tenders think on the health and well being of your loved ones and of yourself through the seasons. Thank yourself for making a healthier version of a childhood treat and remember to enjoy this dinner with your hands... no utensils required when you invite your inner child to dinner!

Taco Bake

Maybe it is typical of me, but I almost always have the ingredients for a quick taco dinner in the house. There is usually a pound of ground meat in the freezer and a can of beans in my pantry. And of course my cabinets must always be fully stocked with boxes of mac and cheese because, well, you just never know when you are going to need it! So here is a quick steamy recipe made with ingredients I, like so many of you, almost always have on hand.

Ingredients

2 boxes Macaroni and Cheese dinner (rice mac and cheese works too)

1 lb. ground beef or turkey

1 can red kidney beans

1 Tablespoon chili powder

1 Tablespoon cayenne pepper

1 teaspoon paprika

1 teaspoon salt

1 teaspoon pepper

1 teaspoon dried cilantro or parsley

1/2 cup water

1/2 cup low fat sour cream

1/2 cup pepper jack cheese, shredded

1/2 cup cheddar cheese, shredded

Sliced Jalapenos (optional)

Directions

Preheat oven to 425. In a large skillet, brown meat. Drain. Add water, taco seasoning, beans, chili powder, and cayenne pepper. Lower heat and let simmer, stirring occasionally, about 15 minutes. Meanwhile, cook macaroni and cheese dinner to package instructions. In a large bowl combine macaroni and cheese dinner, and sour cream. Stir until blended. Spoon macaroni and cheese mixture into the bottom of an oven safe ceramic (or glass) baking dish. Top with ½ of each of the cheeses. Spoon meat and bean mixture on top of macaroni and top with remaining cheeses. Sprinkle sliced Jalapenos on top. Cover and bake for 15–20 minutes at 425. Serve piping hot from the oven.

Magickal Notes

Although you can enjoy this gooey cheesy casserole any time you like, it is particularly a good dish to eat around Imbolc. To celebrate the first of the Fire celebrations, since we cannot always be lighting bon fires in our back yards, hot food is the next best thing. We welcome the transformative fire and the warming of the Sun back to the world through the food we share. Light some orange candles as this dish bakes in your oven to call upon the power and light of the sun.

Sausage Pasta

This recipe is taken right out of my first self-published cookbook, Cucina Aurora Kitchen Witchery Cookbook. It is one of my favorites and so easy I thought it would be perfect for this chapter. I have whipped this dish up for unexpected company and everyone is always very happy when they leave the table. This is best made with sweet Italian pork sausage, but turkey sausage works just fine and is a healthier option. And for my vegetarian friends, soy sausages work well too!

Ingredients

4 links Sausage crumbled and out of the casing
1 Tablespoon olive oil
3 cloves garlic, sliced thin
1 8oz. can tomato sauce
1 cup water
1 Tablespoon garlic powder
1 teaspoon dried oregano
1lb. box Rotini pasta (or other curly pasta)
Pinch coarse ground black pepper
1/2 cup grated Romano cheese

Directions

Cook pasta to package instructions. Meanwhile heat olive oil in large a large skillet and cook crumbled sausage until browned. Add garlic and cook until tender. Add tomato sauce, water, oregano, and garlic powder. Simmer until sauce is reduced by about a quarter. Drain pasta. Add hot pasta to sausage mixture and toss well until coated. Toss with Grated Cheese and serve warm. Top with more grated cheese and fresh cracked black pepper if you like.

Magickal Notes

Sausage is a great way to add zest and variety to your everyday routine. So often, life—and food—take on a ho-hum feeling. Sausage, spicy or not, can add an element of welcome change and a breath of something new. Variety is something we all need now and then. When you cook this meal try adding to that energy by wearing something you would not normally wear: a brightly colored top or a new hair style. Try something new and learn how wonderful variety can be.

Baked Pork and Underworld Apples

Submitted by Joshua Graham, Rome, GA

Around Samhain, Apples are in large supply everywhere. In my home growing up we would go apple picking every October and never be able to finish the abundance of apples we brought home; so many of them got fed to our back yard squirrels. Joshua has another wonderful use for them in this recipe to honor the Sacred Dead.

Joshua says:

"I come from the foothills of North Georgia. In the South, it is common to rush over to someone's home if you hear they have had a death in the family. You clean for them, you help them receive out of town guests, you do everything so they can just grieve; most importantly you bring food. For about a week after the death, friends and family stop by and drop off food for the bereaved. This tends to be my dish to bring. It is different from the fried chicken, casseroles, and quiches that normally show up, and the process helps me in my grieving process. I also take the time to make this when a member of the Beloved Dead has been on my mind. I can do the brining the night before and cook the meal when I get home the next day. For me, it helps stay in the moment with them.

"Not only does the brining process tenderize the meat, but it allows me to bless the meat with water and salt. I use peppercorn for protection and rosemary for memory.

"Nutmeg is a Jupiter spice with protection energies. I tend to make this Dish when working with the Honored Dead, for Dumb Suppers, and on the anniversaries of the deaths of Beloved."

Ingredients

large, watertight container
1 gallon of water
1 gallon of apple juice
2 cups of sea salt
1 cup of mixed peppercorns
7-8 sprigs of fresh rosemary
2 lbs. pork tenderloin
2 Tablespoons of vegetable oil
2 Tablespoons of Honey mustard
1 cup breadcrumbs
2 large apples cored and sliced 1/4 in thick rings
1 Tablespoon Brown sugar
1 Tablespoon of nutmeg
1 cup of apple juice
3 Tablespoons apple cider vinegar

Directions

Pour all the water and apple juice into a large plastic container or stew pot. Set aside.

Make the brine: In a large sauce pot bring to boil 4 cups of the water and apple juice mixture. Add salt and stir until completely dissolved. Remove from heat and add peppercorns and rosemary. Let liquid cool to room temp. Submerge tenderloin completely in liquid, and allow it to soak one hour per lb. of pork. After the meat has soaked place it in the refrigerator for at least an hour. Remove meat from the brine liquid and dispose of all liquid. Let meat rest about 10 minutes. Preheat oven to 450.

After meat has been allowed to sit, heat oil in a large skillet over medium heat.

Brown all sides of the meat in the pan and remove from heat. Rub tenderloin with mustard, and then roll in breadcrumbs. Use roasting sheet or make three or four aluminum foil rings and place them on baking sheet in a row, setting tenderloin on top of the rings

Bake until meat reaches an internal temp of 150 degrees, or about 15 min. While the meat is baking sprinkle apple rings with sugar and nutmeg, and fry on med heat in the same pan the pork was browned until soft and starting to caramelize. Remove meat from oven, turn apples onto low, and let rest for 5 minutes. Place apples on a plate and add a slice of pork on top; garnish with sprinkle of nutmeg.

Magickal Notes

Apples are a food that connects us to the Goddess. A truly Witchy food in my opinion. When you cut an apple in half horizontally it reveals a pentacle hidden within. And in this recipe it is used to celebrate the sacred dead. If you are making this recipe for a specific person, passed or living, place an image of the person in your kitchen. Make sure you place it somewhere that you will see it while making this dish. Light a candle for the dead at the beginning of the preparation of this meal and dedicate your work to them. If you did not know the person who has passed and you are making it honor of someone else's loved one be sure to write that person's name down and place it in your line of sight while cooking.

Chapter Three: Pantry Magick

Baby Makin' Banana Bread

Submitted by Adam Sartwell, Temple of Witchcraft founder and Virgo Minister

Banana bread is one of the easiest and most fondly thought of home baked goodies in the world! The smell of it baking in the oven will get anyone out of bed in the morning. I like to serve mine warm from the oven with a little honey butter and a cup of tea. I am pretty sure most people have made this type of quick sweet bread at some point in their lives, but this is a great story!

Adam says:

"When my older brother and his wife were in the mind to have kids, I asked them both if they really wanted children. From the twinkle in my eye I could tell my sister-in-law knew I meant that I would do magick for them to help them get with child. She said yes they wanted children. So I turned to a recipe I have used to make banana bread for years, but with an altered intention. I blessed the egg for fertility for my sister-in-law and the two bananas for my brother before mixing them into the batter. I stirred the batter clockwise, visualizing the child they would have being healthy. I lit a green candle for fertility on the stove as I baked the bread. Nine months latter I had my first nephew. I have used this spell to get my second nephew, too. That is how this recipe got its name. So you need to be very particular with your intentions when you make this (or any other) recipe!"

Ingredients

1 egg
1 cup sugar
1/2 teaspoon baking soda
2 teaspoons baking powder
1 1/2 cups flour

1/4 cup melted butter

2 ripe (almost brown) bananas, mashed

1 teaspoon salt

Directions

Preheat oven to 375 degrees. Spray a loaf pan with cooking spray. In a large bowl, mix all ingredients together. Pour batter into prepared loaf pan and bake for 45 minutes. Don't cook it longer than that. Test it with a toothpick or thin knife in the middle. If it comes out clean, the bread is done.

Magickal Notes

One of the greatest things about this recipe is that, at any given time, most people have most if not all of these ingredients in their homes. Easy, quick and delicious! But what we don't usually realize is that these everyday items hold so much magick! Bananas, one of the most popular foods in our country are packed with masculine energy. Energetically charging bananas with male fertility energy just amps up their power. Adam also mentioned he charges the egg with fertility for his sister-in-law. This is great because eggs are already a fertility food so when the specific intention is set into this recipe it is naturally very powerful. Draw a symbol on the top of the bread before baking as well. An egg shaped symbol or perhaps a male and female symbol together to bless the union for a child. Be sure not to do this, or any spell or spell recipe without the consent of those involved. We would not want anyone to get pregnant who does *not* want a baby!

Corn Mother Bread

Submitted by Matooka Moonbear, Manchester NH

Corn bread is a staple in many homes and many cultures. Corn is an ancient food the peoples of the Americas have to thank for long years of prosperity, growth and nourishment. It is fitting that we eat it so often and it is found in so many different dishes.

Matooka says:

"This is done ritually to the Corn Mother. I offer each egg, one to the Maiden, one to the Mother, and the last to the Crone. The molasses, maple syrup and honey are offered to the mixture at the end honoring the sweetness of life in each aspect of Goddess. I then offer the complete mixture to the seven directions prayerfully and pop it in the oven. I like to use organics when possible. The flour can be substituted though it really changes the consistency and flavor."

Ingredients

1 cup Cornmeal
1 cup all purpose flour
1 cup milk
1/4 cup vegetable oil
1 teaspoon salt
4 teaspoon baking powder
3 eggs
1 Tablespoon molasses
1 Tablespoon maple syrup
1/2 Tablespoon honey

Directions

Preheat oven to 400 degrees. Spray a 9-inch round or square cake pan with cooking spray. Combine all ingredients in a large bowl and stir until moistened. Pour batter into pan and bake 20-30 min or until toothpick comes out clean in center. Bread should be full, lightly brown.

Cornmeal Cookies

Submitted by Matooka Moonbear, Manchester NH

Ingredients

3/4 cup butter

3/4 cup sugar (or brown sugar)

1 egg

1 1/2 cups flour

1/2 cups cornmeal

1 teaspoon baking powder

1/4 teaspoons vanilla

1/2 cup raisins (optional)

Directions

Preheat oven to 350. In a large bowl, mix butter and sugar. Add egg and beat well with an electric mixer on medium speed. In a separate bowl, blend dry ingredients then add them to butter mixture. Mix well until all ingredients are combined then drop dough on greased cookie sheet by rounded teaspoon full. Bake 10-15 minutes until lightly brown. Remove to wire rack to cool completely.

Magickal Notes

The magickal properties of corn are vast. Corn holds solar energy and masculine energy due to its shape. Ruled by the Sun, Corn is a huge part of many harvest rituals or in honor of Harvest Gods and Goddesses. In both of these recipes corn meal is used as the main ingredient. Corn brings with it prosperity for the year to come and is a wonderful offering to any Gods or Goddesses, especially during Sun/Fire festivals and harvest times. Because it has so many magickal uses, be sure to have clear intentions when working with corn in any form.

Chapter Three: Pantry Magick

Zucchini Bake "Quiche"

Submitted by Beth Moondragon, Ayre, MA

So you have a pot luck brunch you need to go to and totally forgot until right now. What to do? If you have some pancake mix, veggies and a bit of grated parmesan cheese you are all set to make this one-pan baked dish!

Beth says:

"This zucchini bake is based on a recipe that was posted in the Providence Journal over 20 years ago. I grow fresh zucchini in the garden and love to cook with it. I have adapted and changed this recipe, adding in things like mushrooms, and onions... and it's always a favorite at parties!"

Ingredients

3 cups zucchini, thinly sliced
1 cup fresh mushrooms, sliced
1 cup pancake mix (such as Bisquick)
1/2 cup onion, chopped
1/2 cup parmesan cheese
1 clove garlic, chopped
2 Tablespoons parsley
1/2 teaspoon salt
1/2 teaspoon garlic powder
Dash of oregano
Dash of pepper
1/2 cup vegetable oil
4 eggs

Directions

Preheat oven to 350°. In a large bowl mix all of the ingredients. Pour the mixture into a lightly greased deep dish pie plate. Bake for 45-50 minutes until the top is lightly browned.

Magickal Notes

Zucchini is a popular food for many of us. It is easy to get your hands on, flavorful, and a great way to sneak veggies into tons of meals. It is also a hearty plant that grows in the back yard gardens of many witches. But zucchini is also one of those great masculine foods. This would be another great fertility recipe. Bless each egg with female energy and fertility and then the zucchini with male energy. Make sure to do this before you slice up the zucchini and before cracking the eggs. Although zucchini is in season at the end of the harvest season, toward August and September, this dish would be very appropriate to share for Beltane festivals or and fertility rights in Spring.

Crunchy Jam-Stuffed French Toast

Submitted by Allura, Salem, MA

Sometimes, I wake up late on a lazy Sunday morning and crave a big breakfast. These special and far between days are dear to my heart. They are followed by spending the day watching old movies and snuggling up on the couch, or a long afternoon nap with a kitten curled up at my feet. But they all start with a big breakfast. Allura offers a recipe for stuffed French toast perfect for just such mornings!

Allura says:

"If you have a large electric or stovetop griddle, you can probably cook all 6 pieces at once; if not, you can cook in batches and the French toast will hold for up to about 40 minutes in the oven with no ill effects on its crunchy coating. In addition to maple syrup or jam, garnish possibilities include confectioners' sugar, sliced bananas, fresh berries, whipped cream, or even a scoop of ice cream."

Ingredients

4 ounces cream cheese, softened

1/3 cup jam or preserves (your favorite flavor)

Pinch of Salt

12 slices high-quality white sandwich bread

2 eggs

1 cup milk

2 Tablespoons sugar

1/2 teaspoon vanilla extract

3 cups cornflakes, crushed

4 Tablespoons unsalted butter

Directions

In a small bowl, mash together the cream cheese, jam, and a tiny pinch of salt until just combined (streaks of jam are fine). Spread on 6 slices of bread, and top with the remaining 6 slices, pressing gently to form sandwiches.

Adjust the oven rack to the middle position and heat the oven to 300 degrees. Have on hand 2 shallow dishes, such as pie plates. In the first dish, beat the eggs, milk, sugar, and vanilla until uniform. In the second dish, place the cornflakes.

In a large nonstick skillet over medium heat, melt 2 Tablespoons of butter and heat until it stops foaming. Dip both sides of 3 sandwiches in the batter to coat thoroughly, and then dip in cornflakes, patting them over the entire surface to form an even coating. Place them in the skillet, and cook until deep golden brown on both sides, about 4 minutes on the first side and 3 ½ minutes on the other.

Transfer to a baking sheet and place in the oven to keep warm. Wipe any crumbs out of the pan, repeat the process with the remaining 2 Tablespoons of butter and 3 sandwiches, and serve at once, garnishing as desired.

Magickal Notes

The magick in this recipe comes not only from the intentions you put in but what flavor of jam you choose. Since this is totally up to you, you can truly make this French toast suit whatever your magickal needs are. Use strawberry to attract love, raspberry to help with stamina, blueberry for peaceful energy, even peach for passionate energy. The possibilities are endless!

Cider-Glazed Canadian Bacon

Submitted by Allura, Salem, MA
Adapted from Ken Haedrich's Country Breakfasts *(Bantam, 1994)*

Seems this recipe for Canadian bacon would be just perfect alongside Allura's Stuffed French toast!

Ingredients

3/4 cup apple cider
2 teaspoons maple syrup
1 teaspoon butter
12 slices Canadian bacon (about 8 ounces)
Pepper

Directions

In a large nonstick, nonreactive skillet, bring the cider to a boil; continue until it reduces by about two-thirds and thickens slightly, about 4-5 minutes. Add the maple syrup and butter, swirl the pan to blend, reduce the heat to medium, and add the bacon with as little overlapping as possible. Cook until bacon is heated through and liquid is syrupy and glossy, occasionally turning bacon with tongs, about 3 minutes. Season with pepper to taste, and serve at once.

Magickal Notes

Bacon is a food that has been around for a long time. In Medieval times the pig was an important staple as one of the only animals raised specifically for its meat. Pigs were a sign of prosperity and wealth and still hold that energy today. The term "to bring home the bacon" is a great reminder of the prosperity properties of pork. Simmering this bacon with the apple cider and maple syrup sweetens the prosperity. Make this dish to draw money or prosperity into your life. Ask for a raise or a better paying job while you cook with clear intentions.

Chapter 4:
Witchy Entertaining

"Laughter is brighest where food is best."

– Irish proverb

Some look at the idea of having to play host or hostess as a huge undertaking. We scramble around making the house as clean as it can be, lighting scented candles and putting out the "good" towels. It is funny how my home is never cleaner then when there are guests visiting. Fresh flowers in colorful vases are laid out and even the vacuum tends to work overtime picking up as much cat hair as it can manage!

There is a thread of what I like to think of as Sacred Hospitality when it comes to having guests in my home. Whether it is my in-laws staying over for the weekend, a weary musician comrade playing a local convention or just a cup of tea to catch up with a friend I have not seen in a couple of weeks, there is an overall ritual that goes into having people over your home.

The idea of Sacred Hospitality is not unknown to people. To me it is the notion that when you open your home to people they feel comforted, joyful, and peaceful. But there is also the ritual we go through when we are having guests. This is not just for them, but also warms our hearts to know we have made their favorite meal, or given them respite from a long journey. Knowing we have provided someone with a good time and, for our purposes, a good meal is very rewarding. Memories are made around meals or, more specifically, meals shared with those we love. Everything from campfire cookouts to four course meals shared at holidays hold memories and rituals.

This idea does not just stay in the home, but is brought with us to every loved one's home we visit, every group gathering we go to and every potluck meal we share in! This chapter is really the heart and soul of this book. The idea for this compilation came out of one such potluck in the Temple of Witchcraft where the food was so wonderful and the shared hospitality so great; someone said "Hey, we should write this stuff down!"

Chapter Four: Witchy Entertaining

Perfect Potato Salad

Imagine my joy when, on a recent camping trip, a dear friend brought a huge bowl of potato salad. I gobbled it up and on my third helping complimented her on the great dish. She laughed and said "Well, you'd better like it! It's *your* recipe!"

Ingredients

2 lbs. red potatoes cut into bite-sized cubes (washed but
    not peeled)
3/4 cup light mayonnaise
2 Tablespoon deli-style mustard
1/2 yellow onion, chopped fine
3–4 slices bacon, cooked crisp and crumbled
2 hard boiled eggs, chopped into 1/4" pieces
1 Tablespoon blue cheese salad dressing
1/4 cup fresh diced chives
Salt & Pepper to taste

Directions

Boil Potatoes in a large pot on medium heat for 30-40 minutes or until potatoes are easily pierced with fork. Be careful not to overcook. (While potatoes are cooking you can prep other ingredients if necessary.) Drain potatoes and place in a large bowl. Combine with all other ingredients being sure to coat potatoes evenly. Cover and chill for at least an hour or overnight before serving. Serve alongside your favorite grilled entrée!

Magickal Notes

Potatoes are one of those rare foods available and in season just about all year! Remembering always, potatoes are for grounding and keep us connected to the earth. While washing these potatoes think of roots running from your feet to the

Earth. Envision yourself planted in ground. Imagine the cool dirt soothing your feet in the heat of Summer. Share this chilled side dish on hot days to remind you of the soothing coolness of the earth where these potatoes grow.

Three Bean Chili

Don't let the name fool you. Yes, there are three different kinds of beans in this chili, but there are also two different kinds of meat. Bison is my favorite for making chili. It is tender and flavorful and very healthy for you. And although it is a little pricey, most supermarkets are selling it now. This recipe makes a huge pot of chili, perfect for cook-outs, potlucks, camping trips, and leftovers. I almost always have leftovers and put it in the freezer. It is what we call our emergency chili reserve. This chili is so good, I make a huge pot and bring it on our camping trips. It is a favorite of the Pagan rock band Featherscale after they play a gig!

Ingredients
1 lb. ground turkey
1 lb. ground bison (or 95% lean beef)
1/2 large Spanish onion, diced fine
3 cloves garlic, minced
1 green jalapeño pepper, diced *very* fine
2 8 oz. cans organic fire-roasted diced tomatoes
2 15oz. cans crushed tomatoes
1 15oz. can red kidney beans, drained
1 15oz. can pinto beans, drained
1 15oz. can black beans, drained
2 Tablespoons chili powder (or more to taste)
1 teaspoons smoked paprika (or regular paprika)
Pinch cayenne pepper
1 Tablespoon dried cilantro
Pinch sea salt and black pepper to taste

Directions

In a very large sauce pot brown meat with onion, garlic, and jalapeño pepper. When meat has cooked through add tomatoes, kidney beans, pinto beans, black beans, and spices. Stir and bring to a boil. Once boiled lower heat and let simmer for an hour or more. Serve with 1 ounce grated low fat cheddar cheese on top.

Magickal Notes

This recipe has tons of different magickal attributes. Your intention and energetic needs determine how you use this recipe. Beans are associated with wealth and prosperity. This three bean chili promotes these energies in your life. Spice it up a bit with the jalapeños and add a dash of cayenne pepper and you are firing up for a hot spike in your life. Depending on your intention this could go many different ways. If you are focusing on your job you may be line for a promotion, or a raise. If you are trying to heat up your sex life, focus on the love properties of the tomatoes and the heat from the pepper. To kindle health, friendship, or family togetherness call up on the turkey and bison for their energy.

Pears and Brie

I have told this story a bunch of times but it seems appropriate to tell it again. In 2010, I was honored to be asked to cater the first Feast of Hecate at the Temple of Witchcraft. Although I had a set menu in mind when I invoked Hecate into my kitchen she came in, put her feet up and stayed with me for days. She inspired me to make this dish of baked brie and pears. It was a huge hit and people still talk about it. Being that until that night I had not ever even tasted brie before, and had no idea how to cook it, I can only believe I have the Goddess Hecate to thank for the inspiration of this dish. I hope you and your guests find it as amazing as we did on that night we feasted in honor of Hecate.

Ingredients

1 large wheel of brie cheese (extra creamy if you can find it)

3 pears

1 teaspoon lemon juice

3 Tablespoons honey (local to your region is best)

2 Tablespoons cinnamon

1 cup candied walnuts

Directions

Slice pears thin and place in a large bowl. Drizzle with honey. Add cinnamon, and lemon juice. Stir gently being sure not to damage the pear slices, until all are evenly coated in honey and cinnamon. Cover and refrigerate overnight.

Preheat oven to 350 degrees. Cut Brie into wedges and arrange them to look like the same wheel they looked like before you cut it up on a large baking sheet (preferably a round pizza sheet if you have one). Cover the Brie with the pear mixture and any juice that has developed in the soaking process. Cover loosely with foil and bake for 15-20 minutes or until gooey and pears are soft. Top with candied walnuts and serve warm. Note this reheats well so if you are bringing it to a friend's for potluck, pop it in the oven for 10 minutes just to heat it through, if necessary.

Magickal Notes

Hecate is a very present Goddess. She comes when you call and she inspires when you least expect it. Until cooking for her feast I was not familiar with working with her personally. Since then, she is welcome in my home and in my kitchen whenever she pleases. This recipe was of course inspired by her but is suitable for any and all Goddess rituals and even full moon rituals. The brie, shaped in a wheel, can represent the moon or the wheel of the year, whatever serves your purposes. The three pears are for the Maiden, the Mother, and the Crone. Before you cut them up carve a small symbol or a word into them to bless them with these aspects of the Goddess and the Moon. While cutting them up envision the Goddess in that phase of life.

Zucchini Bread

Submitted by Sandi Liss, Butler, NJ

Zucchini is one of those veggies people love or hate! But with the right sweet bread recipe even the staunchest of zucchini snubbers will gobble up an entire loaf. This would be a great recipe to make in the morning if you have overnight guests. The smell of spiced bread in the air is a sure way to gently wake the soundest sleepers

Sandi says:

"This recipe definitely celebrates the harvest, no matter which one you choose. You can also make this bread ahead of time and freeze extra loaves. They keep quite well in a zippered plastic bag. I don't remember where I got this recipe; I've had it so long. I've shared it with a couple of friends who make it all the time. They've changed the name to Sandi's Zucchini Bread though.

"I am the owner of SoulJourney, New Jersey's longest, continually-operating metaphysical store. I am experienced in solitary and coven work, and advises customers on stones, candle magick, and pendulums, just a couple of my passions. I am a certified Astrologer, hold my Master's degree in Natural Healing and continue working toward my PhD, and have achieved my Master level in Usui, Shambala, and Animal Reiki. I currently hold the Treasurer position for D2Care, the Deaf Dog not-for-profit organization (*www.d2care.org*), and am also Secretary for my local business association. I am avid motorcyclist, reader, animal rights advocate, and also love to travel. I share my life with my significant other—with whom I share a passion for cooking—and my two deaf dogs in northern New Jersey."

Ingredients

3 eggs

1 cup vegetable oil or olive oil

2 cup sugar

2 1/2 cups shredded raw zucchini

2 Tablespoons cinnamon

1 teaspoon salt

1 teaspoon baking soda

1 teaspoon baking powder

3 cup sifted flour

1 cup nuts (optional)

Directions

Preheat oven to 350 degrees. In a large mixing bowl, beat the eggs until foamy. Beat in the oil and sugar. Add zucchini, cinnamon, salt, baking soda, and baking powder and mix well. Blend in flour. Fold in nuts if desired.

Pour into two greased loaf pans and bake for one hour or until the loaves start to separate from pan on sides. Cool in pan for 10 minutes.

Magickal Notes

This is a great recipe to celebrate the late harvests. Zucchini is in season starting in July all the way through October in some places. Local Farmers markets are the best for picking up huge zucchini. This vegetable is used magickally for masculine energy and sex magic. You may want to serve this to a couple who are romantically involved or call in the Horned God as you make this dish to bless the harvest.

"Between the Worlds" Curried Pumpkin Soup

Submitted by Steve Kenson, recipe by Newt & Reed

Sometimes a dish just evolves. It becomes a part of the event itself. We all have that dish we make that we bring to other people's homes or that is requested of us to bring to an event. So much so that we look forward to things like "Uncle Joe's Chocolate Chip Surprise" or "Sally's tomato Salad".

Steve says:

"This recipe has a history that starts with my first year attending Between the Worlds, a festival for queer pagan men. Back then, we had a pot-luck meal and the whole community contributed. Newt and Reed made a version of this soup and it was so good I *had* to get the recipe!

"Later, I began making it myself for coven and festival events because it's easy, vegetarian (even vegan, if olive oil and just coconut milk are used in place of butter and cream) and so yummy! Amongst coven members, Newt and Reed's recipe became known as 'The Soup' (definite article) and I was expected to bring it to every feast, if I knew what was good for me!"

Ingredients

1/4 cup butter or margarine
1/4 cup flour
2 Tablespoons curry powder
1/2 teaspoon red Thai curry paste
1 can (15 oz.) solid pack pumpkin
6 cups vegetable stock
1 cup half and half
1 cup coconut milk

1 Tablespoon garlic

1 Tablespoon salt

1 teaspoon ground black pepper

1 Tablespoon cinnamon

1 teaspoon cloves

1 teaspoon ginger

Directions

In a large sauce pan melt the butter or margarine over medium heat and add flour, curry powder, and curry paste. Blend to make a roux. Add 1/2 cup vegetable stock and mix well. Add pumpkin slowly, stirring to blend evenly. Add remaining vegetable stock and stir until smooth, allow soup to simmer for 15 minutes. Add seasonings and spices to taste. Add a pint of coconut milk or half and half (or a mixture of both), and allow soup to heat through before serving. You may want to garnish the soup with a sprinkle of cilantro or parsley and a few toasted pumpkin seeds.

Magickal Notes

Pumpkin is another one of those harvest foods we all look forward to during the year. We wait for the weather to cool just a little in September and just before the leaves start to change it is pumpkin season again! What a great way to celebrate the changing seasons with friends to enjoy this soup made of pumpkin with a kick of curry. Pumpkin is a very feminine food ruled by the Moon. The roundness of the pumpkin brings to mind the fullness of the Goddess at Harvest season. Pumpkin brings fourth healing and prosperity. Share this soup with those whom you wish good health and good fortune.

Savory Sustenance Scones

Submitted by Debra Domal, Urbana, IL

Scones are, in my opinion one of the best treats out there. Tender, crumbly, and not too sweet, these little lovelies can be served at any meal any time of day! Debra gives us one of the nicest savory scone recipes I have ever seen.

Debra says:

"This is one of my favorite and most magickal scone recipes. Bringing together the properties of basil, mint, and lemon these scones are soothing for the stomach and the spirit. A remedy for loss of appetite and an opportunity to release and transform a situation one can no longer "stomach," working with these ingredients can restore a sense of abundance, and with it, the desire to feed both body and spirit with healthy and sustaining things."

Ingredients

3 cups unbleached all-purpose flour

1/2 cup of sugar

Grated zest of 2 small-medium lemons

1 Tablespoon baking powder

1/2 teaspoon baking soda

1/2 teaspoon salt

1 1/2 sticks cold unsalted butter, cut into small pieces

1 cup cold buttermilk (or any kind of milk made sour with a few drops of lemon juice or white vinegar)

Juice of one lemon

1/2 teaspoon dried mint

1/4 teaspoon of dried basil

Directions

Preheat oven to 400 degrees.

Line a large baking sheet with parchment paper.

Combine flour, sugar, zest, baking soda, baking powder, herbs, and salt in a medium bowl.

Cut in the butter and mix in till it becomes crumbly. Add buttermilk and lemon juice.

Turn over dough onto lightly floured surface. Knead with your hands until the dough comes together.

Divide dough in half and pat into two pieces each about 7" across. Cut each into 6 wedges.

Place on parchment paper and sprinkle with extra sugar if you want sweeter scones. Bake for 20 to 25 minutes until golden brown. Makes 12 scones. Best served warm.

Magickal Notes

Basil is not only a wealth herb, but also a love, abundance, and protection food with an overall soothing energy. Mint helps in digestion as well as drawing in money. Lemon is the great purifier. Debra sums it up very nicely here:

"As you prepare the dough, set your intention on the situation or feeling you wish to transform. Feel the heat from your hands transform the butter and flour and release the aromatic healing properties of the herbs. While it is always best to work with herbs that you have grown and dried yourself, any quality ingredients you have blessed and charged with your intention will be fine.

Chicken Florentine Risotto

Submitted by Beth Washington, Ayre, MA

I have personally had the pleasure of camping in the mountains of NH with Beth Moondragon and some other dear friends now referred to as the "Ghetto Crew". It was my pleasure when the time to share potluck feast came around and I took a bite of some wonderful mushroom risotto goodness! Around the campfire I said to my husband, "*Wow*, you have got to try this! It is great!" When Beth said it was her contribution to the feast I was thrilled to know I could get the recipe!

Beth says:

"This chicken Florentine risotto is a recipe built from several different recipes all found on the Internet. I looked up risotto recipes, took about five different ones, and then put together a recipe with all of the things I like. This has become a family favorite, especially with my son. Everyone in the family knows how to make this now. It's easy to make, has a wonderful flavor, and even tastes good as a leftover."

Ingredients

1 lb. chicken, cubed

2 shallots, minced

1 lb. fresh mushrooms, sliced

1 teaspoon Rosemary, ground

Pinch salt (I use a cranberry/rosemary salt)

Pinch Black pepper

3 Tablespoons olive oil

2 cups chicken broth

3 cups vegetable broth

2 cups uncooked Arborio rice (risotto)

1 8oz. package frozen chopped spinach, cooked

3 Tablespoons scallions, chopped

10 oz. chevre (goat cheese)

Directions

In a large sauce pan combine the chicken broth and vegetable broth and bring to boil. Lower the heat to keep it warm, but not boiling. Cover. In another large pot put the olive oil and heat on high. Add the chicken, shallots, mushrooms, rosemary, salt and pepper, and cook until the chicken is cooked, and moisture from the mushrooms is almost gone. If too dry, add a little more olive oil. Lower the heat to a little warmer than medium. Add the risotto and stir until the risotto is coated. Add one cup of the broth mixture and stir occasionally until the liquid is absorbed. Add another cup, and stir until absorbed, and continue in this manner until all of the broth is in the risotto mixture. This process will take about 20 minutes. Once all of the broth is absorbed, add the spinach, the scallions, and the Chevre, stirring until the Chevre is completely mixed in, giving the risotto a creamy texture. Serve warm.

Magickal Notes

Risotto is one of my favorite foods. It is a short rice grain but has a huge capacity to absorb liquid. This is what gives Risotto its creamy texture. Because is it a rice grain Risotto is actually a prosperity food. Since this dish requires a bit of constant stirring, visualize prosperity coming into your life while you stir. Stir in symbols like a money sign ($) into the risotto as it cooks. The spinach in this dish is also a money food and will help to energize the prosperity magick here.

Bacon Fried Corn

Submitted by Lindsey Turner

This is a recipe I would not have thought of at all. I picture sitting around a picnic table in the heat of a July afternoon, when watermelon is ripe, eating this dish alongside a plump hot dog!

Lindsey says:

"I have two recipes I make for all the potluck dinners we have during the year at our fire department. The first is a side dish I call fried corn. I use an electric skillet to prepare this because you can cook it all in one pan and it's easily transported."

Ingredients

1 lb. bacon cut into one inch pieces

2 small cans mushrooms, drained

2 large cans golden kernel corn, drained
  (or use 1 large package of frozen corn)

1 teaspoon garlic powder

1 teaspoon salt

1 teaspoon pepper

1/2 teaspoon cayenne pepper (or to taste)

Directions

In a large skillet, on medium heat (or in an electric portable skillet) cook bacon until crispy. Add the mushrooms and corn and stir to coat with bacon grease. Add garlic powder, salt, pepper and cayenne pepper. Cook until evenly heated and most of the liquid has evaporated. Serve Hot.

Magickal Notes

Corn. What would America be like without it? Corn is one of those foods available to us in every form all year round. It is one of those life sustainers that are staples in so many of our lives. But because it is so common we often take it for granted. Corn is packed full of Sun and Fire energy. Make and eat corn to celebrate the harvest season or to encourage the great Sun and all his power into your home. Share Corn dishes with those you love to blanket them in protective warmth of Sun energy.

Spa-kini

Submitted by Random Al Askendir Xtranj, Reno, NV

Although there is meat in this recipe, those who are health conscious will be thrilled because it is just full of veggies. And for those vegetarians this recipe can be made without the meat and still would be hearty and delicious! And it is gluten-free because it does not require pasta! This is a great one children and adults will both love. I think this would go over wonderfully at any and all gatherings of a Pagan and Non-pagan nature alike!

Random Al Askendir Xtranj says:

"I'm a 48-year-young; single male eclectic Pagan, Scorpio, Moon in Taurus, Capricorn Rising, and Venus in Scorpio Retrograde. When I was 12 my Mom said: "Here's the money for shopping and from now on you're going to be doing the cooking also." I learned quickly. A few years later I managed to attend Job Corps, originally for building maintenance, but when 'Corps Support' week came along, it convinced me to switch to 'Culinary Arts'. I'm a large guy, and I love eating. Thus, I also love cooking.

"This recipe is based on my Grandfather's spaghetti recipe (I just switched out zucchini for the noodles.) I once took this to a local Pagan potluck, and was swarmed and blessed by all the men as it was the only meat dish. When you arrive with it, the men will rejoice!!"

Ingredients

4 lbs. Zucchini, peeled and chopped into small pieces

2 Tablespoons butter

4 large white onions, chopped very fine

1 bunch celery, de-stringed and sliced thin

1 pound mushrooms, sliced thin

4 8oz. cans of tomato sauce,

1 Tablespoon each dried oregano, marjoram, rosemary, and thyme

2 lbs. ground beef (at least 80% lean)

1 lb. of mild cheddar cheese, grated

Salt to taste

Directions

In a large pot bring 6 cups water to a boil. Add the zucchini and let cook until almost mushy. Meanwhile, in a large skillet heat butter. Add onions and sauté until translucent but do not brown. Add the celery and cook until tender. Add the mushrooms and cook 5-10 minutes until liquid is released. Empty skillet into a large bowl and cover tightly. Set aside.

In a medium saucepan at medium heat, cook tomato sauce up to just boiling. Add the herbs and let simmer. Meanwhile, in a large skillet over medium heat, cook ground beef until no part of it is pink, drain the grease off. Drain the cooked zucchini, and mash it a bit. Uncover the mixing bowl and pour the heated sauce in, mix well. Add in 1 cup of cheese and mix well. Cheese will begin to melt.

Pour the cheese and vegetable mixture into the drained zucchini pot, mix, and add in the cooked, crumbled hamburger. Mix to coat. Add salt to taste. Add remaining cheese and mix well. Cover the pot, and let stand for 10 minutes before serving, or cover and take it to a pot luck feast.

Magickal Notes

This recipe has so many wonderful ingredients it is hard to just pull out one thing to focus on. Keep in mind the zucchini has masculine energy due to its shape. Perhaps it is that energy that fuels this dish and we could serve it to celebrate the Horned God or the Sun! Random Al Askendir Xtranj offers his own thoughts on the magick of this dish:

Chapter Four: Witchy Entertaining

"It tastes massively better and works better for the health of those who will eat it when 'Reiki energy' is broadcast into the pots and pans while things are cooking. Cooking this food can be done ritually, to even greater effect. In past versions that I have done, Air Elementals like to be involved in slicing, Water Elementals in mixing, Fire, of course, love cooking, and Earth Elementals like to be involved with the mushrooms, cheese, and the herbs. I'm not saying that this is when you should summon them, I mean that after they have been summoned and the actual cooking has begun, you can invite them from their quarter to pay special attention to this part for the magickal good and health of the result. Stopping after you grind a herb in your hand, thanking Earth for it, and kissing the air above it before you sprinkle it in makes everything nicer. And the Elementals seem to continue having a vested interest in making sure that the food gets to the event, even after the sacred space they were involved in is brought down."

Chapter Four: Witchy Entertaining

Blaze's Crock-pot Shrimp Creole

Submitted by Gail Wood, Freeville, NY

For me "spicy" and "shrimp" just go together. I love a good jambalaya or skewers of shrimp dusted with Cayenne pepper and maple gaze. This recipe from Gail could not be simpler! Take everything and put it in the crock pot and it cooks itself!

Gail says:

"One of the more common nutritional myths is that shrimp need to be shunned because they are a source of bad cholesterol. This has not only been disproven, but this delicious fresh and salt water crustacean is nutritionally beneficial as a source of omega-3 fatty acids, B-12 and niacin. Shrimp is rich in the minerals of iron, zinc and copper."

Ingredients

1 1/2 cup chopped onions

3/4 cup chopped celery

1 clove garlic minced

1 28-ounce can whole tomatoes

2 8-ounce cans tomato sauce

1 teaspoon salt

1 teaspoon sugar

1/4 teaspoon paprika

3-6 drops Tabasco Sauce

1 lb. fresh shrimp or 16-ounce package frozen shelled shrimp, rinsed and drained

Directions

Combine all ingredients except shrimp in the Crock-pot and stir to blend well. Cover and cook on low for 7-9 hours (high for

3-4 hours). During the last hour, turn the Crock-pot to High, add shrimp, and cook for one hour or until the shrimp is pink.

Magickal Notes

Shrimp, like so many shellfish are closely associated with Aphrodite and increasing sexual desire, especially in women. The paprika and Tabasco sauce in this recipe are also are what would considered foods of lust. You know, "spice" things up a bit!

Gail offers more insight into shrimp:

"In the web of life, shrimp are tiny creatures that help maintain a healthy ecosystem by preventing an algae build-up in an aquarium or underwater living space and by getting rid of debris. As we consume shrimp, we can imagine it magically preventing a build-up of harmful blockages and debris in our systems. The tasty combination of vegetables and spices in this Creole dish reminds us life is not only to be lived beneficially but also enjoyed for all the spice it can give us!"

Seven Seas Christmas Stew

Submitted by Allura , Salem, MA

Although I come from a traditional Italian family, fish was never really a big thing for us at the holidays. My grandmother would make tons of meat, pasta, antipasti and cookies but the old world tradition of Christmas Eve fish dinner was somehow lost on my family. It was most likely due to the ten grandkids complaining about how we all just wanted ravioli! As I got older I started to celebrate this timeless tradition and every year when we celebrate Christmas Eve with our Christian families I like to cook a big meal and include a new and interesting dish from the Sea. Allura gives us a great one to try here for Christmas holidays, and Yule Celebrations!

Ingredients

2 Tablespoons olive oil

3 garlic cloves, minced

1 28 oz. can Italian plum tomatoes

2 8 oz. bottles clam juice

1 teaspoon dried parsley flakes

1 teaspoon dried basil leaves

1/2 teaspoon coarsely ground black pepper

1/4 teaspoon crushed red pepper

2 dozen littleneck clams

1 dozen mussels

3/4 lb. large shrimp

1/2 lb. sea scallops

1/2 lb. cleaned squid

1/4 lb. flounder fillet

1/4 lb. cod or scrod fillet

1 loaf Italian bread (optional)

Directions

Heat oliver oil an 8-quart Dutch oven or saucepan over medium heat until hot, but not smoking. Sauté garlic until tender, but not browned. Stir in tomatoes with their liquid, clam juice, parsley flakes, basil leaves, black pepper, and crushed red pepper; bring to a boil. Reduce heat to medium-low; cover and simmer 30 minutes, stirring occasionally.

Meanwhile, with a stiff brush, scrub clams and mussels under running cold water to remove any sand; remove beards from mussels. Shell and devein shrimp; rinse with running cold water. Rinse scallops with running cold water to remove sand from crevices. Cut squid crosswise into 1/2 inch thick slices. Cut flounder and cod into 1 inch chunks.

After sauce has simmered 30 minutes, add clams and mussels to Dutch oven. Over medium-high heat, cook, covered, until shells just begin to open, stirring occasionally, about 5 minutes. Stir in shrimp, scallops, squid, flounder and cod. Cook 1 minute or until fish flakes easily when tested with fork and shrimp and scallops turn opaque throughout.

Magickal Notes

Ever wonder why Italians are known for their food and their capacity to love? Here it is! This stew is just overflowing with love, and passionate energy. The shellfish are very closely linked to love and lust. Remember lust can not only be sexual but can be for life, for beauty, for family and even for great food! Couple the fish with the tomato sauce and let it simmer to a stew like we have here and you can be sure you have a dish that reflects the love you feel for those you hold dear. Make sure to visualize those you adore as you make this stew. For even more magick, carve their names or initials on the shells of some of the clams and mussels. Remember to use this recipe not to draw love, but to celebrate that which you already have!

Lady Moondancer's Slamming Barbecue Beans

Submitted by Ruth Pace

So many of our pot luck type events happen in the warm months where the barbecue is the center attraction. What better than a cookout in a good friend's back yard, with children running through sprinklers and different dishes covering the table with tastes from twenty different kitchens? These beans are a great fit for that or any picnic setting!

Ingredients

2 cans your favorite brand plain barbecue beans

2 teaspoons brown sugar

2 Tablespoon honey

2 Tablespoon maple syrup

1 Tablespoon molasses

Directions

In a large pot on medium heat pour beans. Add brown sugar, honey, maple syrup and molasses. Stir well. Simmer on low heat until sauce is nice and thick. (about 15 minutes). Stir frequently as you don't want to burn it. Serve warm.

Magickal Notes

Sweet foods attract Fairies. In fact, when I am cooking with sweet ingredients I almost always leave an offering to the Fae and thank them for being present in my kitchen. While stirring the honey and other sweet and sticky ingredients into these beans hit some chimes or ring a bell. Invite the Faerie Spirits into the kitchen. But be sure to ask them not to cause any real mischief! When Fairies run amuck in your kitchen things could get sticky! Then leave them a drop or two of honey, syrup, and molasses out in the yard by a flowering tree to thank them for their presence.

Chapter Four: Witchy Entertaining

Chapter 5:
Libations

"Wine is bottled poetry."

– Robert Louis Stevenson

Can you think of anything more fun than a drink with friends? Sometimes "getting together for drinks" is an evening unto itself. How many times have you stepped out in your nicest outfit to meet a first date for "drinks"? We see glamorous celebrities in upscale bars sipping pink drinks out of fancy fluted glassware and we can't help but admit we like to do the same from time to time.

I myself am not much of a drinker. But a magickal libation has been part of the practice for pagans and non-pagans alike. Many spiritual traditions incorporate wine, ale, or mead into rituals. In ancient times, water was not consumed. Ale or mead had to be made so that the water could be sterilized and made safe to drink. Ale or beer was the beverage at every, and all, meals. It was used for offerings to the Gods and Goddesses, and shared at rituals. Wine is another largely used beverage, seen as the divine gift of gods like Dionysos, much as mead was the draught of inspiration of the Norse gods.

It seems only natural in a cookbook about magickal foods we would include a chapter on magickal libations. Not all such beverages are alcoholic. Just like spell recipes involving food, the ingredients and the intention that go into a beverage are influential. It is from the intention and the purpose of the person working with the ingredients that the magick is brought out of the ingredients. When it comes to alcoholic beverages it is important to note that, even in magickal works, moderation is key. Too much liquor can hinder your ritual or magickal work.

Chapter Five: Libations

Traditional Wassail

The word *wassail* literally translates to "To Your Health!" an exclamation said while drinking this warm beverage. It was enjoyed in the ancient times at many Winter celebrations. Most people think "to wassail" means to carol or sing, as in "Here we come a Wassailing, among the leaves so Green". But really this drink was named for the toast that was commonly made while drinking it. A toast would be made not only to friends and family but in the woods to the trees, to the ancestors, to the spirits and to the fairies. I have made this every Yule for years. When they walk through the door on a cold Winter's night they are greeted by the smell of cinnamon and apples and a warm cup of wassail!

Ingredients

1 gallon apple cider

1/2 cup brown sugar

2 Tablespoons honey

8 sticks of cinnamon (one for each Sabbat in the Wheel of the Year)

1 large orange, cloved (pierce the orange with cloves in a symbol if you like, such as a pentacle)

1 large apple (cut in half side ways to reveal the pentacle within)

6 whole nutmeg

6 whole allspice

Pinch ground ginger

1 cups rum (optional)

Directions

Put all ingredients in a large sauce pot. Cover, leaving the cover just askew so a bit of steam comes out. Simmer on low heat for no less the one hour. If you choose to let it simmer longer, stir every hour to make sure fruit does not burn on the bottom. Ladle into large mugs for serving. You can garnish each mug with a cinnamon stick, or put an apple wedge at the bottom of each mug before ladling and provide a spoon so the apple can be eaten when the Wassail is finished.

Magickal Notes

Traditionally a Yule drink, this hot beverage was shared with friends, family, and neighbors. Offerings were made to Mother Earth and to all her creatures with a portion of wassail poured directly into the Earth on the Longest Night, the Winter Solstice. Because it takes a while on the stove to make wassail, you can put it on in the afternoon and let it heat until your guests arrive for the feast. Notice how the aroma of spiced apples and cinnamon fill your home and make your kitchen a warm and inviting place. Before your meal, offer some wassail to the nature sprits around you and pour some at the base of a tree or in a wooded area.

Be Well Tea

I have never claimed to be an herbalist expert, but as a Kitchen Witch, I do work with culinary herbs quite a bit. One of the things I love is tea. I actually have a bit of an obsession if you ask around. In my house a popular drink I make when someone is not feeling well is what I call "Be Well Tea". It has the ability to clear up clogged sinuses and sooth a cough. This is real magick in a cup for anyone with a cold.

Ingredients

2 oz. dried echinacea

2 oz. dried eucalyptus

2 oz. dried elderberries

2 oz. dried stinging nettles

3 oz. dried peppermint

Directions

Put all dry herbs in a large jar. Cover and shake the jar up until all herbs are evenly dispersed. Distribute desired amount into tea strainer or cheese cloth bag for tea. Boil water and pour into large mug with prepared tea bag or strainer. Steep for 10-15 minutes. Add honey or raw sugar if desired. For best results to help get over a cold, drink at least three cups a day.

Magickal Notes

While visiting an herbalist friend in Maryland my husband caught a bad cold. She immediately went into her garden and cut some nettles and peppermint. She brewed them up with elderberries and that was the beginning of my love of this tea. When I got back home I ran right to the herb store and got all of these herbs. Nettles, echinacea, and eucalyptus are all strong immune system boosters, the elderberries help with congestion, and the peppermint adds a nice flavor to cover up the somewhat strong taste of the other herbs. Make this tea with a heaping Tablespoon of honey and you will be well on your way to feeling well again in no time!

Life Force Elixir

Submitted by Christopher Penczak, Temple Founder and Sagittarius Minister

Christopher and I have shared many a four-hour lunch together and in that time I have had the pleasure of enjoying his sense of humor and his lust for life. When we started talking about what recipe he wanted to submit for this collaboration it was clear this was the perfect chapter for one of his concoctions!

Christopher Penczak is the co-founder of the Temple of Witchcraft and the author of many books on Witchcraft, magick and spirituality. He's been a menace to the kitchen and a potion maker since he could crawl, and his parents were delighted to find a spiritual purpose to his love of little bottles and mixing crazy things together and insisting people drink it. Today he has a healing and spiritual counseling practice in Salem, NH, where he administers herbal remedies and flower essences to help people work through their physical, emotional, mental, and spiritual issues to gain a greater sense of wholeness and connection. For more information, visit *www.christopherpenczak.com.*

Christopher says:

"Everybody who knows me knows I'm not a very good cook, but I *do* like to make potions. I've been making them since I was a child and, on some level, I think I've always been called to the art of potion making. But thankfully I've stopped using things found under the sink to bubble and froth and stick to more edible ingredients. Even more fun than making magickal potions are the magickal drinks that can be taken for fun, outside of the context of a serious ritual. Some of the most social potions you can make are cordials. Cordials are herbal extracts, often sweetened, believed to have a medicinal virtue to increase the constitution, aid digestion, bolster energy, or enhance your mood. They make excellent after dinner drinks, and I've enjoyed quite a few around the campfire of a pagan festival late at night, watching the Moon and stars. Today they are usually called liquors, as the medicinal virtues of alcoholic drinks are downplayed, but most witches know better. That's why I prefer the term cordial. Unlike wines, there is no fermentation taking place, so they can be easier for a novice drink maker, as you don't have to worry about yeast or any other fermenting issues. Many traditional alchemical elixirs are made in a very similar way, with alcohol and water extracting the colors and properties, then separating and recombining parts of the formula to create a new, more powerful blend. It's in that spirit that I created this cordial for both its magickal properties and its taste, out of some of my favorite herbs. There is an ingredient for each of the seven planets of the ancients. Each confers a different blessing, and taking them all together creates a balanced harmony, bolstering life force."

Ingredients

3 Tablespoon lemon balm

1 Tablespoon elderberry

1 teaspoon ginger

1 lemon

1 teaspoon lavender

1/2 teaspoon vervain, blue

1/4 teaspoon nettles

3 cups vodka (80 proof or higher)

Canning jar (3 cups or larger)

1 1/2 cups honey

2 cups spring water

Directions

Grind each of the herbs in a mortar and pestle, infusing them with your magickal energy. If you're a modern Witch, the sacred herbal coffee grinder works wonders and is easier on the wrists, though I like the old ways myself. Bless each of the herbs as you place them into the canning jar. Hold the intention of increasing life force, flow, and health as you breathe your intention onto the herbs. Call upon the spirit of each plant to aid you in creating a healthy, life-enhancing drink. If using fresh lemon balm—which I recommend whenever possible, as the plant is flowering with little white flowers—double the amount of lemon balm to 6 Tablespoons. Slice and squeeze the lemon and also bless it and place it into the jar. Pour the vodka over the herbs and fill the canning jar. If your jar has a metal lid, place plastic wrap between the mouth of the jar and the lid and tighten, to prevent the vodka from touching the metal. Most new jars have coated lids, so the plastic is unnecessary. Shake it up and let it steep for at least two weeks, if not longer. Pour out the alcohol and strain it through an unbleached coffee filter, to separate the herbs and lemon from the liquid. Soak the herbs in 2 cups of spring water for three days. Strain the herbs out, and heat the liquid, adding 1 and 1/2 cups of honey slowly to the water, allowing it dissolve. Add the honey water to the vodka extract and let it sit for at least one moon cycle (28 days) before drinking. Shake the mixture regularly during this Moon cycle. It will then be ready to drink as an herbal cordial. If the mixture is not sweet enough for you, you can dissolve more honey and add it to the elixir.

Magickal Notes

Christopher's explanation is extensive! Enjoy!

"In alchemy, one of the most prized herbs is lemon balm, considered the premier herb to gather life force and bolster the life force in humans. Supernatural tales of it completely regenerating the skin, hair and nails are common from alchemical texts. While I can attest to its healing properties, I've found its effects natural and measured over time, restoring vitality and vigor. It's great for when you've lost that twinkle in your eye and want it back. Lemon balm is considered a cure-all. It alleviates headaches and stress, though it isn't really a traditional sedative. It helps calm the stomach, digestion, particularly when you have a nervous stomach. It relieves depression. The spirit of the herb both calms and uplifts, enhancing anyone. The plant spirit is of a helpful and generous nature, wanting everyone to be happy. The latin name for it, *Melissa officinalis,* relates it to the honey bee, also known as the Melissa, as well as the ancient Greek priestesses and attendants known as Melissa. It's quite a magickal herb, associated with the Moon and Jupiter. It brings good fortune. When fresh, this plant from the mint family smells like fresh lemons. Lemon Balm is the main ingredient because of all these magickal qualities to enhance your life force.

"Elderberry is the fruit of the elder tree, another magickal plant. The elder is associated with the Faery Queen, and one must make an offering to the Faery Queen before harvesting wood, flowers, or berries from the plant, particularly if the elder is standing alone. The realm of Faery is both powerful and sometimes dangerous, and proper respect must be given. In folk traditions children were advised not to fall asleep under this faery tree, or else be swept away into the otherworld. Elder is ruled by the planet Saturn, the planet of karma, boundaries and protection. Elder berries are nutritious, and particularly useful in enhancing the immune system to ward off all manner if winter illnesses. It is said that when there is an abundance of elder flowers in the summer, then flu season will be unusually strong that winter.

"Lemon is a great flavoring, particularly to enhance the flavor of lemon balm, which can lose some of its lemony-ness when dried. Lemons are ruled by the Moon, and folk magick uses them to bring love, luck, and psychic ability. If you fear too strong a lemon taste in your cordial, one Tablespoon of lemon peel can be used. A fresh lemon, as opposed to lemon juice, is always preferable.

"Ginger is our spice for the mix, to bring a strong fiery taste to compliment the cooler flavor of the lemon. Ginger is ruled by the Sun, and increases the metabolism, circulation and generally brings "heat" to any mixture. Ginger powder is used in magick for health and wealth.

"Lavender is another herb to compliment the taste, adding a bit of a "flowery" note to the mix. Ruled by Mercury and Jupiter, it brings calm and soothing power to the mix."

"Blue vervain is technically ruled by Venus, but has a lot of Mercurial qualities. This herb helps bring us out of our heads, when we think too much and are not fully enjoying the world around us and the moment at hand. It is said to be a cure for "high-mindedness." Vervain is the witch's herb, used for any magick: protection, love, money, health, and blessing.

"Nettles is our last herb of the mix. Tasting very "green" it is an herb of Mars, as the stingers on the fresh plant indicate the presence of a warrior spirit. Nettles magickally helps protect us, and also increasing our magickal life. It's another faery herb, helping induce contact to the fey folk. Medicinally it is a blood "purifier" with a tonic effect on the body. It relieves inflammation, lowers blood sugar and appears to aid those suffering from hay fever. An herbalist once told me if you don't know what's wrong with a person, start out with Nettle tea and see if they get any better. Nettle can seem to lower blood pressure, so if that's an issue, beware.

"Interestingly enough, this mix of herbs brings excitement to the body, but a bit of tranquility to the mind. Together the concoction is to revitalize the whole self, as the seven planets are associated with the seven chakras in the body and the seven subtle spirit bodies: Saturn - Root/Physical, Jupiter - Belly/Etheric, Mars - Solar Plexus/Astral, Venus - Heart/Emotional,

Mercury - Throat/Mental, Moon - Brow/Psychic and Sun - Crown/Divine."

Chapter Five: Libations

Xochiquetzal Chocolate

Submitted by Gail Wood, Freeville, NY

We all know chocolate is a love food and, in some cases, a sex and passion food. A cup of hot chocolate is something we enjoy on cold nights and after shoveling snow. What most of us don't realize is how long the tradition of hot chocolate has been around, not to mention how sacred the beverage was and still is!

Gail says:

"The following recipe was used in workshops I facilitated on the Goddess, Xochiquetzal. This sensual goddess of love, beauty, and delight was honored in the households by women. She was the goddess of the arts, of prostitutes, and childbirth.

"The recipe is one of the many adaptations of Mexican chocolate. This chocolate is not the chocolate milk you find in the grocery store. It has spice, grittiness, and bite that awakens your senses. There are other recipes and sometimes using block chocolate makes the drink slightly gritty. Some recipes use hot peppers for a strong flavor and smooth aftertaste. Experiment boldly. Whatever recipe you use, let it take hold of your senses and feel the joy of the Goddess through your senses and your pleasure. For all acts of love and pleasure are my rituals."

Ingredients

1/3 cup unsweetened cocoa powder

1/4 - 1/3 cup sugar

1/2 teaspoon cinnamon

1/4 teaspoon nutmeg

1/2 cup hot water

3 1/2 cups milk (or part cream)

2 teaspoons vanilla

dash salt

Pinch Cayenne pepper (optional)

Directions

In a medium sauce pan on medium heat place cocoa powder, cinnamon, nutmeg, and sugar. Add water, stirring constantly for two minutes. Add milk and stir. Continue to heat but do not boil. Beat in the vanilla, salt, and cayenne pepper, if desired. Serve warm. To make a mocha-flavored beverage, add 1 Tablespoon dry instant coffee to dry ingredients.

Magickal Notes

Gail has a great knowledge of this recipe's background and uses.

"Legend has it the plumed serpent god Quetzalcoatl assumed human form and brought a gift from the garden of Paradise; the precious cacao tree. He showed humans how to cultivate the tree, prepare the harvest, and use the beans for his favorite drink, Xocolatl. Since that time, cacao has been combined with different ingredients for many uses such as healing, trance work, comfort, and nourishment. The scientist, Linneaus, named the chocolate tree *Theobroma cacao L,* meaning "Food of the Gods.

"Today, in modern Spanish-speaking households, the making of the chocolate drink is part tradition and part ritual; perhaps the remnant of some ancient worship. A Mexican expression translates as, "To be perfect, a cup of chocolate must be hot, thick, sweet... and made by the hands of a woman." The chocolate is served cold with a cap of foam because the foam is said to embody the spirit of the chocolate and the energy of the person who prepared it. This is another linking of person to person and of body to spirit.

"In our society, chocolate is many things including a comfort food. Its magical properties elevate our sensuality, heighten our happiness, and provide us with a vision of sweet life".

Elemental Martinis
Submitted by Michael Cantone, Salem NH

The following are four recipes for four different martinis I was lucky enough to partake in at a Yule/Birthday party. Michael was there trying out all these recipes and plying the lot of us with tasty magickal spirits! What a night around the bonfire! You will want to make these for every season... there is one for each!

Michael says:

"Alcoholic beverages provide a great way to use magick in food preparation. The ancient word for alcoholic beverages is 'spirits' and that is because of the fermenting process that goes into the production of alcohol. Whether it be beer, wine, vodka, or gin, there is a distillation and fermenting process similar to the steps alchemists and witches use to make tinctures. In this process, sprit is being extracted from plants in liquid form. Above all, this is a fun way to make magickal beverages.

"Following are recipes for elemental martinis. Each recipe is for one drink and can be altered to increase the quantity of drinks being prepared. Although each martini focuses on a particular element, just like in magick in general, each element has all of the elements within it. For example, the base of each martini is vodka. Alcohol corresponds with the element of fire. Most vodkas are made from either potatoes or grain, which correspond to the element of earth. Martinis are made with the ingredients poured over ice which then melts and now we are working with the element of water. So you see, like in Witchcraft, the elements are interwoven."

Celestial Fire Cosmo Martini (Fire)

"The Celestial Fire Cosmo Martini is a great refreshing drink with a bite that can be ingested anytime. The element of fire pierces through the element of water inherent in the cranberry juice.

"Mix the following ingredients into a martini shaker filled with ice and with a 'fire' magickal intent in mind"

Ingredients

One part plain vodka
One part orange vodka
Half part of cinnamon schnapps (I use Goldschlager)
Two parts cranberry juice

Directions

Shake the above mixture and pour into a martini glass. Garnish with a cinnamon stick, a cinnamon candy, or an orange slice.

"Orange and cinnamon correspond to the element of fire while the cranberry juice corresponds to the element of water. The gold flakes in the Goldschlager adds a nice touch of alchemy to the drink. Watch out, two of these and you will think you have discovered the Philosopher's Stone!"

"If one is feeling really creative, replace the cinnamon schnapps with a mixture of ground cinnamon and ginger. Start by grinding fresh ginger with ground cinnamon, ice, and a splash of plain Vodka. Add the above ingredients, excluding the schnapps, to a martini shaker, shake it up and serve in a martini glass. This will provide the same refreshing flavor with fresh herbs."

"And finally, if one is courageous craving a drink of all fire, replace the cranberry juice with a cherry Kool-Aid and a cinnamon potion. Boil cinnamon sticks in a saucepan of water. The water should just cover the cinnamon sticks. Pour the water and sticks into the Kool-Aid. Include in this drink the above ingredients, excluding the cranberry juice, add the ginger and cinnamon mixture to taste. The cherry Kool-Aid corresponds to the element of fire. Two of these martinis and you will breath fire like a dragon!"

Whirling Peppermint Martini (Air)

"The Whirling Peppermint Martini is a refreshing drink that can be served anytime and is also good for after dinner. But watch out, it has a kick. Unlike the previous martini, there is less preparation time. Mix the following in a martini shaker with ice and with an 'air' magickal intent in mind."

Ingredients

One and half parts of plain vodka
One part and half parts chocolate milk
Half part of peppermint schnapps (100 proof Rumple Minze is the kick)

Directions

Shake the mixture and pour into a martini glass. Garnish with a fresh mint leaf, a peppermint stick, or a peppermint patty candy.

"Inhaling the scent of this drink while sipping heightens the air element. The peppermint/mint is the ingredient that corresponds to the element of air and is the most prominent flavor in this refreshing cocktail. For an even more fiery drink, replace the chocolate milk with one part clear chocolate flavored liqueur (Crème de Cacao works nicely). Sip slowly and feel the air and fire elements swirl nicely together"

Melon Fusion Cosmo Martini (Water)

"The Melon Fusion Martini Cosmo is a great martini anytime, before, during, or after dinner. The recipe below is for a mixture of melon and watermelon flavored vodkas but can be altered for one's preference. Mix the following in a martini shaker with ice and with a 'water' magickal intent in mind."

Ingredients

One part plain vodka
One part melon flavored vodka
One part watermelon flavored vodka
Two parts cranberry juice

Directions

Shake the mixture and pour into a martini glass. Garnish with a slice of lemon or lime.

"Melon, cranberries, and lemon correspond to the element of water and together present one a smooth refreshing and loving drink. Replacing the lemon with a fiery garnish of lime makes this a lustful cocktail. Two of these and you will be in love."

Terra Pumpkin Martini (Earth)

"The Terra Pumpkin Martini is autumn in a glass, good anytime, and simple to make. Mix the following in a martini shaker with ice and with an 'earth' magickal intent in mind."

Ingredients

Three parts vanilla flavored vodka
One part pumpkin pie filling

Directions

Shake the above mixture and pour into a martini glass and add a sprinkle of allspice on top before serving.

"For an extra sweet drink, rim the glass with sugar and allspice. Both the pumpkin and allspice correspond to the element of earth. The vanilla vodka provides the sweetness to the drink, like drinking a slice of pumpkin pie.

"There you have it, elemental martinis! Enjoy them, and above all, drink responsibly, and in the company of good friends."

"The Aunts" – Lavender and Honey Infused Wine

Submitted by Ruby Sara

I have never actually attempted to make my own wine. But Ruby Sara's simple and very magickal rendition of this sweet wine is perfect for any of us who have always wanted to try our hand at potion making!

Ruby Sara says:

"I am a poet, essayist, performance artist, and devotee of Dionysos (not necessarily in that order). I am also the editor-in-chief of *The Temple Bell,* official newsletter of the Temple of Witchcraft. I enjoy baking sacred bread and concocting magical wines in the fiercely wild urban Midwest.

"This recipe is an adaptation of an ancient Roman drink called mulsum, which is really just wine sweetened with honey. From my experiments in herbalism and cordial-making, I decided to add lavender to the recipe. Other herbs and spices that work well for infused mulsums are vanilla beans, cardamom seeds, saffron threads, and other spices and edible, aromatic herbs. I've even experimented with a couple of red wine mulsums using coarsely ground black peppercorns or coffee beans! Though the lavender white continues to be a favorite."

"I have been making The Aunts (named for Stockard Channing and Dianne Weists' characters in the film *Practical Magic)* and other honey and herb/spice infused wines for several years. The magic here is the inexpensive and miraculous transformation of some cheap wine into a sweet, magical and delicious potion—good for offerings and great for passing around the bonfire on summer nights. It's ridiculously easy to make and extremely forgiving to those who find measuring things oppressive, but it tastes so lovely that inevitably someone will ask for the recipe, anticipating some elaborate affair involving a secret lab, a golden bridle, three hairs from the chin of a chimera, and the ability to cook. Luckily for me, it actually requires none of these things.

"While I imagine that this brew will keep for quite some time, I have never had a chance to find out. It's always gone in a matter of days!"

Ingredients

(makes two bottles)

2 bottles dry white wine

3-4 heaping Tablespoons dried lavender blossoms

1/4 - 1/2 cup wildflower honey (Remember to support local and organic beekeepers!)

Directions

Find the most inexpensive bottles of dry white wine you can. In a half-gallon mason jar, add the lavender followed by both bottles of wine. Cover the jar and let sit overnight. In the morning, you'll find the lavender has dyed the wine a gorgeous pink color. Strain the wine through cheesecloth into a stainless steel pot and compost the used lavender blossoms. Gently heat the infused wine on the stove at the lowest setting and add honey to taste. Stir gently, making sure to heat the wine only enough to assist in dissolving the honey. When all the honey is dissolved, remove from heat and allow to cool. Transfer the lavender and honey infused wine back into the bottles and re-cork. Enjoy!

Magickal Notes

We see quite a bit of lavender in a witch's kitchen. It is an herb used in many relaxation teas, incenses, and oils. We even notice it in lotions and bath products. But most never really think of this as a culinary herb. I have used it in scones, breads and marinates. Happily I welcome the idea to bring its relaxing energy to a wine that will help mellow heated arguments between lovers, or calm a battered heart.

Ruby Sara says:

"Medicinally speaking, lavender is a brilliant nervine, found in hundreds of recipes and applications for its soothing and relaxing scent. It is also often found in love spells. Likewise, many of the spices listed above are associated with love spells in different traditions, and honey is an age-old ingredient in many spells designed to "sweeten" a lover to you, making this recipe and adaptations thereof particularly well-suited to love magic. In addition, it is an excellent libation or ritual drink for spring and summer celebrations."

Holiday Eggnog

Submitted by Jean Pando, Watertown, MA

Eggnog has never been one of my favorite holiday traditions. That is, until I tried Jean's homemade recipe below. It is thick and creamy with just the right amount of sweetness to ring in the holiday season. This easy recipe gives you no excuse to ever buy supermarket eggnog again!

Jean says:

"The winter holidays wouldn't be complete without eggnog. I formulated this recipe as an easy, delicious alternative to the store-bought varieties. It is actually based upon the instant breakfast drink my mother would sometimes prepare for me at breakfast. Choose fresh, organic eggs and cream for the best taste."

Ingredients

1 1/2 pints all purpose cream

1/2 pint whole milk

7 eggs

2 Tablespoons pure vanilla extract

7 teaspoons sugar

1/8 teaspoon ground nutmeg

2 oz. brandy or rum (optional)

Directions

Combine ingredients in blender; blend on high for 3 minutes or until all are combined and a thick creamy mixture is produced. Pour into tumblers and sprinkle with nutmeg and cinnamon. Can be served chilled or at room temperature.

Magickal Notes

It is no wonder to me that Eggnog is a traditional holiday libation. This drink goes back to medieval England, where the upper class would drink it mixed with brandy on special occasions. Eggs are one of the best fertility foods out there. So to eat—or in this case, drink—eggs can be powerful fertility magick.

At Yule we welcome back the light and celebrating the triumph of Light over Dark. From Yule onward the Sun begins to strengthen and light begins to return. This is time to set intentions and plant the seeds of what you would hope to grow in the coming light. Although the Witch's New Year begins at Samhain in October, many of us still set intentions on December 31st as we let go of the old year and welcome the new one. Drink this eggnog at any of these occasions to have your intentions for the coming year be fertile and grow.

Sangria

Submitted by Allura, Salem, MA

I have a friend who occasionally needs "Emergency Sangria". To some of us this sounds strange, and to others, it is perfectly normal, albeit a bit humorous! Sangria is what I like to think of as a "Party Wine". It is sweet, fruity, and refreshing. Sangria is prefect after a long day at work or when you need a little together time with your friends, particularly when it is a group of women having "girl time." Leave it to Allura, with her light and laughter, to submit these two recipes for a party in a glass! Make up a pitcher of this and see how the laughter flows!

Classic Red Sangria

Ingredients

3/4 cup simple syrup (see following)
2 bottles red wine
3/4 cup brandy
1/2 cup triple sec
3/4 cup orange juice
2 oranges, sliced into thin rounds
2 green apples, cored and sliced thin
2 lemons, sliced into thin rounds

Directions

Combine all ingredients in a large pitcher and refrigerate, covered, two hours or up to two days. Serve over ice. Serves 6-8.

Pomegranate Sangria

Ingredients

3/4 cup simple syrup (see following)
2 bottles red wine

1 cup pomegranate juice

3/4 cup brandy

1/2 cup triple sec

3/4 cup orange juice

2 oranges, sliced into thin rounds

2 green apples, cored and sliced thin

2 lemons, sliced into thin rounds

Pomegranate seeds

Directions

Combine all ingredients in a large pitcher and refrigerate, covered, two hours or up to two days. Serve over ice. Serves 6-8

Simple Syrup

Add 1 cup sugar and 1 cup water to a small saucepan over medium heat. Bring the mixture to the boil so the sugar dissolves. Transfer to a heatproof container and allow to cool to room temperature before using. Simple syrup can be stored in an airtight container in the refrigerator for one week.

Magickal Notes

Intention is everything. Here we have two really wonderful Sangria recipes and although there are magickal correspondences in the ingredients (Pomegranate for fertility and Goddess energy, oranges for Fire energy and to bring in the Sun God) the true magick here is in the person mixing the ingredients together. Your mind should be clear and your heart should be light as you combine these liquids and stir them clockwise in the pitcher. Visualize the laughter and joy of sharing this refreshing libation with kindred spirits around the pool or on the patio. Those sharing the Sangria with you will surely feel the joyful energy you have added with every sip!

Apple Pie Libation
Submitted by Ayrzabet.

Alcohol is generally thought of for celebrations, and relaxation. However, as noted in the beginning of this chapter, it is used as a ritual tool as well. Ayrzabet's recipe is a perfect libation to share at any harvest ritual, particularly at Mabon and Samhain.

Ayrzabet says:

"This is a very potent alcoholic libation we have used at many pagan gatherings. It's smooth going down and really sneaks up on you."

Ingredients

1 qt. everclear (grain alcohol)

1 qt. vodka

2 gallons apple juice

2 gallons apple cider

7 sticks cinnamon

4 cups sugar

1 cup brown sugar

1/2 teaspoons ground nutmeg

1/4 teaspoon ground allspice

1/4 teaspoon ground cardamom

Directions

Mix apple juice, apple cider, sugars, cinnamon sticks, and spices together. Boil until cinnamon sticks lose flavor. Remove from heat and add everclear and vodka. Refrigerate in gallon jugs. Serve chilled.

Magickal Notes

This is a great libation for Harvest celebrations. Apples are used in many divination spells. They hold the protection of the pentacle and the power of the Mother Goddess. In our part of the world, New England, apples are abundant from late August with the height of their perfection in mid-October, all the way until late November. The grain alcohol amplifies the apple with deep soothing warmth from within. Like a hug from the Mother as you pass the chalice during your Harvest Ritual. Celebrate the Mother as Crone, wise and full of love, as you head to the dark time of Winter.

Chapter 6:
Sweets

"Cookies are made with butter and love."

– Norwegian proverb

There are not many who can resist a sweet treat. What is it about desserts that make us turn into giddy children? Even when we are not interested in eating anything but the salad we ordered for dinner we take a glance at the dessert menu and insist we are too full to eat any. But there always seems to be room for a cookie, a scoop of ice cream, or "just a bite" of chocolate.

I learned to love the kitchen and all the wonders it holds by baking. Although I consider myself much more of a cook then a baker, my earliest memories of the kitchen are baking cookies with my mother. Children tend to learn about ovens and ingredients though the power of cookie baking. Even something as simple as crispy marshmallow treats can be the beginning of someone's love of cooking. In this chapter I noticed many things that could have gone in the Heirloom Magick chapter because the recipe was handed down as a traditionally loved dessert.

So many magickal foods fall under the blanket of desserts. Numerous love spell recipes center around chocolate. Chocolate is the ultimate love food. With sexual energy and lust full force, chocolate can be made into cakes, cookies, ice cream, candy, milkshakes, muffins, and sauces. I have even seen full editable sculptures made out of chocolate!

In my opinion sweets have gotten a bad reputation. I would agree that unnatural things, like high-fructose corn syrup, have had a negative impact on the way we eat and think about desserts. But there are more desserts than just the surgery sweets we see in supermarkets. Sweet things, like honey, agave nectar, and maple syrup are keys to love spells and the Faerie realm. The Fey creatures love their sweets. If you wish to invite them into your kitchen leave out some fruit dipped in honey in your yard, or flower bed. Sweets can also bridge gaps in relationships when made with the right intentions. Desserts are a welcome gift to a new neighbor and can brighten a work day.

Confections also give us opportunities to use fruits in different ways. Pie, for example, can be made from just about any kind of fruit. When you bake fruits down, even bitter ones like rhubarb, the sweetness is reveled. Just like in life, when you soften someone, or yourself, you see the true sweetness inside. Cakes, sweet breads, cookies, and candies can be made to feed many and are always the most welcomed and anticipated part of the meal. Head to the kitchen and let yourself get covered in powdered sugar while you enjoy making treats for all to enjoy!

Autumn Apple Crisp

This is one of my absolute favorite desserts. When I teach a class on Kitchen Witchery I almost always bring something with me to feed the class. Last year at an event up in New Hampshire, I made four huge trays of this apple crisp. I served it piping hot as people came in from the rain to learn about Kitchen Witchery. They all left smiling. This recipe keeps in the fridge for up to a week and you can reheat single servings in the microwave easily.

Ingredients

5 large apples (preferably Cortlands) peeled and sliced thin
1/4 cup water
Juice from 1/2 of a lemon

Topping
1 cup flour
1 cup rolled oats, uncooked
1/2 cup butter or margarine, softened
1/2 cup brown sugar
1 Tablespoon cinnamon
1/2 cup chopped walnuts or pecans (optional)

Directions

Preheat oven to 350. Combine apples with water and lemon juice in a deep medium-size baking dish. Set aside. Combine flour, oats, butter, brown sugar, cinnamon, and nuts to form a crumb mixture. Distribute evenly over apples in baking dish. Bake, uncovered 45 min to 1 hour, until edges bubble and top is a deep golden brown. Serve warm with a scoop of vanilla ice cream if desired.

Magickal Notes

In Autumn the air becomes crisp and apples are in abundance. When slicing the apples for this satisfying dessert, notice the crisp sound and be reminded of the crisp breezes of Fall. This traditional food of the Goddess reveals a pentacle when cut horizontally. While this dessert is baking take a deep breath and let the smell of apples and cinnamon remind you of the bounty the Earth offers during this season of Harvest.

Double Chocolate Crumb Cake

Is it just me, or are there never enough crumbs on a crumb cake? Although I have tried and tried to make a "Just Crumb" dessert, apparently the crumbs need a cake to stick to. So after much trial and error here is the best crumb cake recipe I have come up with. It is chocolate cake, with chocolate crumbs drizzled in melted chocolate. If this does not please a picky crowd I am not sure what will!

Ingredients

1 box chocolate cake mix
2 cups flour
1 cup unsweetened cocoa powder
1 1/2 cup sugar
2 Tablespoon cinnamon
Pinch nutmeg
2 1/2 sticks butter
1 cup chocolate chips

Directions

Preheat oven to 350 degrees. Make cake mix to package instructions in a 9x13 cake pan. Bake for 28 minutes. While cake is baking combine flour, cocoa powder, sugar, cinnamon, nutmeg and butter in a bowl and mix with fork. Make sure the butter is in small balls no smaller then a pea size. After the 28min take the cake out of the oven and cover with crumb topping. Bake another 10 minutes. Remove from oven. Let cool 30 min. In a microwave safe bowl, melt chocolate chips in 30 second increments until smooth. Drizzle melted chocolate onto crumb cake. Refrigerate for at least an hour before serving.

Magickal Notes

Chocolate lovers, rejoice! This cake is full of love and passionate energy. Before pouring the cake batter into the pan write the names of your loved ones, intended lover or present spouse in the greased pan. This helps to focus the intention of love for those individuals. Remember as well that cinnamon and nutmeg are sprinkled into the chocolate topping for even more love and a pinch of fire energy!

Lemon Blueberry Bunt

This cake was one I put in the "Spring" section of my self-published book, *Cucina Aurora Kitchen Witchery Cookbook* and people come up and compliment me every time they make it. The lemon blueberry bunt is simple to make because it starts out with a store-bought cake mix. This cake has actually won an award in dessert contests and my father-in-law has been quoted as saying it is "perfect" when I made it for him for father's day. Now it is requested at most birthdays!

Ingredients

1 box lemon cake mix
1 package instant lemon pudding mix
1 cup milk
4 eggs
1/3 cup vegetable oil
Juice from 1 lemon
1 Tablespoon lemon zest
1 cup blueberries

Directions

Heat oven to 350 degrees. Spray a bunt pan with non stick cooking spray. In a large bowl with an electric mixer on low speed, beat cake mix, pudding mix, milk, eggs, lemon juice and oil. Stir in the zest and blueberries. Pour into pan and bake for 50 minutes to an hour until toothpick inserted in cake comes out clean. Cool completely before glazing.

Glaze: Mix together 1 1/2 cups confectioner sugar, and 6 Tablespoons of lemon juice until smooth. Drizzle over the top of the cake. Refrigerate until ready to serve.

Magickal Notes

Few things smell as clean as fresh lemons. The tart citrus is one of Nature's most powerful cleaning agents, and so it cleanses your life and your spirit. Lemon scrubs away tarnish on the soul and refreshes us with an eye-opening scent and a burst of sour sweetness. As you zest the lemon for this recipe, being careful to only get the yellow rind and not the white under skin, use this action to peal away negativity from your heart and mind. Take a deep smell of the lemon as you juice it, letting the juice trickle between your fingers cleansing any remaining negativity.

Strawberry Peach Pie

In Fall we tend to do more baking and cooking then we do in the Summer months. I guess the idea of turning on the oven in heat over 90 degrees can be a bit daunting. But if you make a pie early in the morning before the weather gets too hot you can have the proverbial pie cooling on the windowsill, and your home will smell like fresh picked fruit all day!

Up here, in my part of Massachusetts, I can't drive two miles without seeing a farm or farmers market on the side of the road. They bid me come and enjoy all the fresh summer produce right in my own back yard. Signs that yell "pick your own peaches" and "our own fresh strawberries" temp me as I drive by. Since I love to stop and buy these fruits and there is almost always more than I can eat by myself, this pie uses up the leftovers very nicely!

Ingredients

4 fresh peaches, sliced thin, skin on

1 1/2 cup sliced fresh strawberries

1/4 cup peach preserves

1/4 cup sugar

1 teaspoon cinnamon

1 Tablespoon flour

1 package refrigerated ready pie crust

Directions

Preheat oven to 350 degrees. Line a 9 inch pie pan with pie crust and set aside. In a large bowl, combine all peaches, strawberries, peach preserves, sugar, cinnamon, and flour. Pour into warm pie crust. Cover with another pie crust. Pinch top and bottom crusts together. Poke a few holes in the top of the crust with a fork to vent. Place the pie plate on a cookie sheet to prevent dripping when in the oven. Bake for 30-40 minutes or until top is slightly golden brown. Cool and serve.

Magickal Notes

Peaches and strawberries are two of Earths sweetest gifts in Summer. This pie requires very little sugar because the fruits are full of their own natural sweetness. Both strawberries and peaches hold similar magickal properties. Strawberries are a love food but, more specifically, for increasing passionate love and the desire for it. Strawberries help us to draw this energy into our love lives. Peaches also hold love properties. As a symbol of flesh and desire peaches energy encourages us to give as well as receive love. Putting peaches and strawberries together in this pie creates a recipe that might heat things up in the bedroom!

Gumdrops

Submitted by Edain McCoy, recipe created by Rev. Donald B. Taylor

These little drops of joy can be made in any flavor or color your heart desires. Use your imagination for these and share the experience of making these sweet drops with family members, especially children!

Edain says:

"My father used this recipe long before I was born. Like his father, my father was a connoisseur of confections. He had a wonderful collection of candy recipes he used for fundraisers or for our family winter holiday celebrations. As I searched for unusual recipes for this collection, I realized my family has not made gumdrops since long before my father passed over—a situation soon to be remedied.

"I have been a Witch since 1981. Since then I have studied followed traditions made-in-the-Americas traditions, learning something new and exciting with each. I am a historian, graduate student, a speaker at Pagan festivals, and the author of over 20 books on Witchcraft, magick, and the occult arts. Find more information at my website, *www.edainmccoy.com*."

Ingredients

One package unflavored gelatin

6 Tablespoons cold water

1 cup granulated sugar

1 small bowl granulated sugar (for rolling the finished gumdrops)

3 Tablespoons water

Flavor extracts (your choice)

Food coloring (your choice)

Directions

Mix the gelatin in the cold water and let it set. Meanwhile, boil to the semi-hard stage the granulated sugar and water. Add your choice of flavor extract and food coloring. Pour over the gelatin and mix them thoroughly. Place in refrigerator. When set to the consistency of gumdrops, cut and roll in granulated sugar. Store uncovered in refrigerator.

Note: Do not try to shortcut the flavoring by substituting juices for the 6 Tablespoons of water. Juice disrupts the chemistry of the recipe and they will not set.

Magickal Notes

Edain sums it up nicely by saying:

"By using and mixing food colorings the gumdrops can be made in a color to match your magickal need. You can also be creative with the flavoring. A spicy cinnamon will spark your love life and libido, a gentle vanilla brings you tranquility and beauty, almond brings clarity of mind, and orange awakens the senses."

For some other magickal correspondences you might try: Red food coloring and strawberry flavoring for passionate love, green food coloring and mint flavoring for drawing money, or yellow food coloring and lemon flavoring for purification.

Coconut Fudge Brownies

Submitted by Jocelyn VanBokkelen, South Hampton, NH

There are few sweet treats that make everyone smile like brownies do. Something about a brownie and a big glass of ice cold milk can make your worst day better and a great day fantastic. I was lucky enough to get to try these brownies at TempleFest, a Summer festival organized and run by the Temple of Witchcraft. Jocelyn handed me a moist brownie and I was in heaven! They can be made in a variety of ways to fill your needs.

Jocelyn says:

"My kitchen sometimes runs to not having the 'right' ingredients for things.

Sometimes I really want something so I make substitutes. This started out as "fudge brownies" out of *Better Homes and Gardens New Cook Book* but it's hard to see the resemblance now, and even harder when one goes for a gluten-free version. These can be made gluten-free by using any of coconut flour, rice flour, or almond flour in place of the white flour. I've also used whole wheat flour with success. If you want them more chocolaty, the cocoa powder can be doubled, and slightly less flour used."

Ingredients

1 stick butter
1/2 cup unsweetened cocoa powder
1 cup sugar
4 eggs
1 teaspoon vanilla
3/4 cup flour
1/2 cup unsweetened coconut
1/2 cup chopped nuts (optional)

Directions

Preheat oven to 350 degrees. Spray an 8x8-inch baking dish with cooking spray and set aside.

Melt the butter in a medium saucepan along with 1/2 cup of unsweetened cocoa powder. Turn off the heat and add the sugar, eggs, and vanilla. Mix together. Stir in flour, coconut, and nuts. Pour into baking dish and bake for 30 minutes. Center will still be moist. Do not overcook. Let cool completely before cutting and serving.

Magickal Notes

Chocolate is one of the all time best love foods you can work with magically. When working with chocolate, as with any magickal cooking, you want to make sure you have clear intentions. Before pouring this brownie mix into the pan, write the name or names of your loved ones in the pan with the tip of your finger. Then as you pour the mix into the pan you are "covering" your loved ones with love energy! Remember too that these brownies require coconut. If you choose to tap into the coconut energy, then meditate on the purification of the love for those you will be sharing these brownies with. Perhaps there has been a fight or uneasiness in the relationship. Envision smoothing things out with this person or people. Remember, chocolate is not just for romantic love. This works well to mend any relationship, not just romances.

Peanut Butter Chocolate Pie

Submitted by Sandi Liss, Butler, NJ

Chocolate and peanut butter is one combination we can't get enough of. We see it everywhere from peanut butter cups to children's cereals. The rich flavor of salty sweet peanuts and creamy chocolate are here in Sandi's creation. This is a very fast no-bake dessert everyone will love.

Ingredients

12 oz. cream cheese

1 cup confectioner's sugar

8 oz. peanut butter

8 oz. whipped topping such as Cool Whip

Graham cracker pie crust

Directions

Mix together cream cheese and confectioner's sugar. Add in peanut butter. Add in Whipped topping. Mix together by hand (mixture is very thick). Pour into pie crust and freeze for one hour. Serve cold cut into small slices.

Variations: Use chocolate whipped topping instead of plain, Add in mini chocolate chips or use crunchy peanut butter

Magickal Notes

Although we see the combination of chocolate and peanut butter quite often, we never really realize how magically potent it can be. Chocolate is a love food, but peanuts are actually not nuts at all. They are legumes, or beans. This puts them in the prosperity category of magickal foods. Mixing together the thick pie filling, focus on prosperity or, more specifically, what brings prosperity into your life, your job, your drive, your dedication for your work. Then think about all the things you love about your work. Do this particularly on a day when you are not very happy with your job and refocus your energy on the good things about your work.

Grape-nut Custard Pudding

Submitted by Rama Danu, Salem, NH

I never would have thought to make a dessert pudding out of Grape-nut Cereal! I used to love this cereal as a child because it never seems to get soggy. Leave it to a witch like Rama to figure out a way to take something so simple and turn it into something truly special!

Rama Says this recipe is "Decadence inspired by the Goddess herself!"

Ingredients

10 eggs

1 1/2 cup sugar

1 Tablespoon vanilla extract

1 Tablespoon ground cinnamon

1/2 gallon whole milk

1 cup grape-nut cereal

1/2 cups sugar

1/4 cup cinnamon

Directions

Preheat oven to 350 degrees. Grease or spray with cooking spray a 1/2 hotel tray pan (12x9 and 2 1/2 inches deep). Put Grape-nuts in a large bowl and set aside. Scald milk: stir milk briskly over medium heat almost to a boil, but do not let it boil. Pour scalded milk over grape-nuts and let sit for about five minutes. With a wire whisk, beat together eggs, sugar, and vanilla in another large bowl. Combine with grape-nut mixture. Pour into the prepared pan.

Sprinkle generously with cinnamon and sugar. Set in a pan of hot water and bake until a knife inserted one inch from the center comes out clean, about 75 minutes (convection oven time). Top with whatever fruit makes your heart happiest: strawberries, blueberries, or apples, to name a few.

Makes about fourteen good size-sized servings.

Magickal Uses

Grape-nut cereal is made of whole grain wheat and barley flour. Rama soaks them in this recipe in whole milk. This is one of the most important steps in the magick of this recipe. Soaking the wheat and barley nuggets in warm milk softens them, like the love of the Great Mother Goddess nurtures and softens us. Milk is a nurturing food full of mothering energy. This dish is best served warm to celebrate the Goddess. Depending on the time of year you can top it with different fruits to best call in different faces of the Goddess. In the spring, use cherries or strawberries for the Maiden, and in the fall use apples for the Crone.

Buckeye Candy

Submitted by Kim, Ohio

Another recipe featuring the classic combination of chocolate and peanut butter. These are just as good if you use creamy almond butter instead of peanut butter. They are very easy to make and would be a wonderful project to share with children on a rainy day!

Ingredients

2 lb. bag confectioner's sugar

1 1/2 sticks butter, softened

3 cups creamy peanut butter

about 1 lb. dipping chocolate

Directions

Mix powdered sugar, butter and peanut butter in a large bowl with your hands until dough forms. Roll into small balls. Use a toothpick and dip balls into melted chocolate, leaving the top exposed. Store in refrigerator.

Magickal Notes

These candies are called "buckeyes" because they are meant to resemble the eyes of a grown male deer. For our own magical purposes we can take that idea and envision the great Stag, the Horned God, and all his wisdom as we make these simple treats. When you take a bit of this sweet confection, ask the Horned God to see as he sees, with compassion and light. Ask that he help you focus through your third eye and see what might not be visible to all.

Crunchy Date Blondies

Submitted by Beth Moondragon, Ayre, MA

We see a lot of chocolate in the world of desserts. I am a huge fan of it myself, but sometimes I need a break. Beth has two wonderful chocolate-free recipes made with naturally sweet dates in the blondies and tart cranberries in the coffee cake. These add welcome variety when chocolate seems a bit too heavy.

Beth says:

"I took the Witchcraft series of classes with Christopher, graduating Witchcraft V several years ago. I am currently studying shamanism with Steve Wilson. I teach classes and lead rituals for Aquarius Sanctuary, and I am a crafty person, making many different pagan items, and selling them as a vendor at several events.

"I've never really thought about being magickal in the kitchen, though I do like to grow my own vegetables and herbs, and enjoy the magick of nature in them. I do like to cook special dinners, things people like, and bring people together to share meals.

"These crunchy date nut blondies were an adaption of chocolate chip bars, made for my neighbor who on occasion comes to my rescue and plows snow from my driveway. He and his family are allergic to chocolate, so I substituted dates. I'm allergic to walnuts, so I make them with pecans instead."

Ingredients

1 1/4 cups packed brown sugar

1/2 cup butter, softened

2 eggs

2 teaspoons vanilla

1 1/2 cups flour

1 teaspoon baking powder

1/4 teaspoon salt

1 cup chopped dates

1/2 cup chopped pecans

Topping

1/2 cup packed brown sugar

2 Tablespoon butter softened

2 Tablespoon light corn syrup

2 Tablespoons milk

1 cup flaked coconut

1/2 cup chopped pecans

Directions

Heat the oven to 350 degrees.

Lightly grease a 13x9-inch baking pan. Set aside. In a large mixing bowl, combine 1 1/4 cups brown sugar, and 1/2 cup butter. Beat with an electric mixer at medium speed until light and fluffy. Add the eggs and vanilla. Beat at medium speed until well blended. Add the flour, baking powder, and salt. Beat at low speed until well blended. Stir in the dates and ½ cup pecans. Spread the mixture evenly in the prepared pan. Bake for 20-28 minutes, or until golden brown. Remove from the oven and cover with topping.

Topping: Set the oven to broil. In medium mixing bowl, combine all topping ingredients, except the coconut and pecans. Stir until well blended. Stir in the coconut and 1/2 cup pecans. Spread the topping evenly over the blondies. Place under the broiler with the topping 4 inches from the heat. Broil for 1-2 minutes, or until the topping is bubbly.

Cool completely before cutting. Makes 32 blondies.

Magickal Notes

In my opinion, dates are one of the most unsung, under used foods out there. They are sweet and chewy and make a great base for many desserts. I have done everything with dates from drizzle them with honey and cinnamon to stuff them full of goat cheese and sliced almonds. Beth uses them in this recipe as a substitute for chocolate chips. Dates help us to stay connected to spirit; our own, and others around us. This recipe is very magickal! Dates help strengthen any spiritual work you are doing. Eat these before meditation or hypnosis.

Cranberry Cake

Submitted by Beth Moondragon, Ayre, MA

Beth says:

"I created this recipe from scratch. This is a family favorite I make at home when I feel like making something special. The cranberry cake is loosely based on a pineapple upside down cake, but heavily adjusted and changed. I made it once as the wedding cake for a hand fasting, and it was a hit. It continues to be a favorite during the holidays with family."

Ingredients

1 1/3 cup sugar

1 1/4 cups all-purpose flour

1 1/2 teaspoon salt

1 1/2 teaspoon baking powder

1 teaspoon grated lemon peel (orange peel can be substituted)

1/4 cup butter, softened/melted

1/2 teaspoon vanilla

2 eggs, slightly beaten

2 cups fresh cranberries, chopped

Directions

Preheat oven to 350°

Grease bottom of cake pan with 1 Tablespoon of butter or line the bottom of the pan with parchment. Mix together all of the dry ingredients. Mix in all of the remaining ingredients until the dry mixture is moistened. Pour into the prepared cake pan. Bake 40-50 minutes.

Let stand to cool about 20 min. Flip the cake onto a plate while it is still slightly warm. Frost the top of the cake with the cream cheese frosting, allowing it to drip down the sides. Chill.

Cream Cheese Frosting

Ingredients

1 pkg. (8 oz.) cream cheese – softened

5 cups powdered sugar

3-5 Tablespoons water

Directions

Using a mixer on low, combine the cream cheese and powdered sugar until well blended. Add water until the frosting is the desired consistency. Extra frosting can be kept in the refrigerator for 2-3 weeks in a sealed container.

Magickal Notes

I simply love cranberries. They have a sweet tartness that is unmistakable. They mix well with citrus flavors like in this cake with lemon peel. But they are also a protection food. Make this cake with the intention of protecting those who will eat it, specifically if you are making it like Beth did for a handfasting or other occasion. Write the person's name in the pan when you are greasing it with the intention of protecting them from harm or illness. This makes a perfect Autumn dessert if you are inclined to make it for your Mabon celebrations. Then use the intention of general protection against the harsh winter months.

"Next Best Thing"
Submitted by Lindsey Turner

Is this dessert over rated with the name of it? No! It is decadent and wonderful! Layers of chocolate and whipped cream topping on a nutty crust, what could be better?

Lindsey says:

"The dish I take to the potluck dinners I got out of a book by Christine Feehan. She took a collection of recipes from her readers, so this is not my dish originally but it's so good I had to share. The original name was "Next Best Thing to ... Feehan novels" I shortened it to just "Next Best Thing." This can be made almost completely sugar free by using a sugar substitute, low-fat cream cheese, sugar-free pudding, and low-fat or sugar-free Cool Whip.

Ingredients

1 cup flour
1 cup chopped pecans
1 stick butter
8 oz. cream cheese
8 oz. whipped topping, such as Cool Whip
1 cup sugar
1 large vanilla instant pudding mix
1 large chocolate instant pudding mix
3 cups cold milk
8 oz. whipped topping
1/2 cup chopped pecans (optional)

Directions

Preheat oven to 350 degrees. In a food processor or blender mix flour, pecans, and butter until crumbly. Spray a 9x13-inch pan with non stick cooking spray. Evenly press this mix into the pan. Bake for 15 minutes, take out and let cool.

Mix cream cheese, whipped topping, and sugar in the food processor until creamy. Spread this evenly over the warm crust layer. Whisk vanilla pudding mix, chocolate pudding mix and milk together until stiff and spread this over the cream cheese layer.

Top with the last 8oz. of whipped topping and sprinkle with pecans for garnish. Refrigerate until serving. Store in the refrigerator up to a week.

Magickal Notes

Fluffy, creamy, and rich, this dessert is perfect for a girl's night in. Chilled to perfection it has an almost cheese cake texture in the middle and it is beautiful sliced and served with a side of strawberries. Cream cheese, just like all cheeses, helps to lift your heart and brings joy into your home. Paired here with the sweetness of the layers of chocolate pudding and the pecan crust this cheese's power has been amplified to bring light-heartedness and almost giddy attitudes. Try it for lifting spirits and be ready to be in for a long night of giggles!

Grandma's Christmas Brownies

Submitted by Elaaine Stormbender

Yes, we already have a brownie recipe in this chapter, but, like I said, I am a huge fan of brownies. I could not see having only one brownie recipe when they are both so wonderful. Elaaine has shared with us a recipe with German Chocolate. I can only imagine how wonderful it was for Elaaine to make these brownies with her grandmother when she was a child. Serving these with marinated cherries and a dollop of vanilla ice cream would make a fantastic German Chocolate Sundae... mmmm the possibilities of a good brownie recipe!

Ingredients

4 ounces German sweet chocolate

5 Tablespoons butter

3 ounces cream cheese

1 cup sugar

3 eggs

1/2 cup plus 1 Tablespoon all-purpose flour, unsifted

1-1/2 teaspoon vanilla

1/2 teaspoon baking powder

1/4 teaspoon salt

1/2 cup walnuts, coarsely chopped

1/4 teaspoon almond extract

Directions

Melt chocolate and three Tablespoons butter over very low heat, stirring constantly. Set aside to cool. Blend the remaining butter with the cream cheese until softened. Gradually add a quarter-cup sugar and blend until light and fluffy. Stir in one egg, one Tablespoon flour, and a half-teaspoon vanilla until blended. Beat remaining eggs until fluffy and light in color.

Gradually add remaining three-quarter-cup sugar, beating until thickened. Fold in baking powder, salt and remaining half-cup flour. Blend in cooled chocolate mixture. Stir in walnuts, almond extract, and remaining teaspoon vanilla. Measure one cup of chocolate batter and set aside. Spread remaining batter in a greased 9-inch square pan. Pour cream cheese mixture over the top. Drop measured chocolate batter from Tablespoon onto the cheese mixture. Swirl the mixtures together with a spatula to marble. Bake in a pre-heated oven at 350 degrees for 35 to 40 minutes. Cool and cut into bars or squares.

Magickal Notes

Swirly brownies! Using these brownies with the marble cream cheese mixture in a magickal way is easy. They help us represent balance. Notice the way the cream cheese mixture cuts right through the chocolate, showing a beautiful marble. Let this serve to remind us there can be no light without dark and no dark without light. Even try drawing symbols into the marbling as you go. Infinity symbols, hearts and spirals are the easiest and infuse the energy of those symbols right into your brownies.

Dark Fruit Cake with Brandy

Submitted by Alix Wright, Salem, NH

Alix and I became friends after the very first TempleFest. After the festivities we all went out to dinner and Alix got stuck sitting next to me and my husband at the end of the table. Since then we make time to have tea and laughs as often as both of our busy schedules allow. She has told me on many occasions of her infamous Brandied Fruit Cake. This is *not* your typical holiday fruitcake that comes in a tin and is stored above the refrigerator and thrown away by Spring. This cake soaks in Brandy for no less than two weeks. There is so much Brandy in this recipe I almost put it in the libations chapter! Can't wait until Yule comes around and Alix makes it again!

Alix says:

"I usually make my cakes the weekend after Thanksgiving and they're done by Yule, but as long as you have two weeks to add the extra brandy you're fine."

Ingredients

3 lbs. seedless raisins

1 lb. Sultana raisins

1 lb. candied pineapple

1 lb. candied cherries

3/4 lb. mixed fruit

1/4 lb. candied papaya

1 lb. dates

1 cup brandy (more for marinating the cakes later)

1 lb. blanched almonds

2 1/2 cups flour

1 tsp baking powder

1 tsp salt

2 tsp nutmeg

2 tsp cinnamon

1 tsp ginger

1 tsp allspice

1 tsp cloves

1 lb. butter

2 cup white sugar

12 eggs

1/2 cup sherry

1/2 cup strawberry jam

2 tsp vanilla

Directions

Chop all the fruit into very small pieces. Put all the fruit in a very large bowl and pour the brandy over fruit mixture. Cover tightly and let sit for a day. The next day add two thirds of the nuts. Sift the dry ingredients over the fruit and nut mixture and mix thoroughly. Use your hands so that you can get the dry ingredients mixed in well. In another bowl, cream the butter until it's very soft. Gradually add the white sugar. Beat in the eggs one at a time.

Add sherry, strawberry jam, and vanilla. Add the wet ingredients to the fruit mixture. Mix thoroughly with your hands. (You may need to split this into two bowls.)

If you're adding almonds, heat the rest of them in the oven until they're piping hot and then add them last. Mix thoroughly.

Line bread pans with buttered parchment paper. Pour the mixture into the pans. The weight of the mixture will weigh down the paper, making sure the corners are tightly down. Bake at 250 degrees for 4 hours.

When the cakes have cooled take them out of the pans. Wash pans and put a layer of plastic wrap in with enough to wrap over the top of the cake. Put the cake back in and spread about 1 Tablespoon of brandy over it. Seal the cake in the plastic wrap.

Every other day turn the cake over and add the brandy. Reseal in the plastic wrap. Do this for no less than two weeks. Serve at room temperature.

Magickal Notes

There are so many magickal ingredients with wonderful energies in this recipe it is hard to single out just one to focus on. What really stands out here magickally is the time, preparation and, above all, patience these cakes take. Starting these cakes right after Thanksgiving and keeping them moist, marinating them every day for a month building up to the holiday celebrations of Yule and Christmas and even New Years takes dedication. Use this time to reflect on what you hope to bring to your life in the coming year. Every time you baste the cake in brandy put into the cake an intention for the coming year. When you finally eat this cake you will be taking in all those good intentions as well as a delicious dessert!

Cranberry Solstice Cookies

Submitted by David Salisbury, Washington, DC

Cranberries are to Fall as watermelon is to Summer. Once the air cools and the smell of autumn leaves is in the air cranberries make their triumphant return. Here in New England we have cranberries by the barrel full; cranberry scones, cakes, sauces, chicken, stuffing. The list goes on and on. David shares with us his vegan recipe for tart and sweet cranberry cookies.

David says:

"This recipe is one of the very first I've ever tried making myself. Since I was young, my grandmother used to let me go to town with mixing up random baking ingredients and cooking them in the oven just for fun. Usually they came out mush but sometimes we'd get something edible out of it. This recipe started as a random conglomeration of festival ingredients that I like to have around the winter holiday months. Because of that, they remind me that wonderful things can be born of our fearless creativity and love.

"I am a Priest of the Firefly House, a nature-based church in Washington DC. I have been practicing the Craft for 11 years and have been vegan for nearly as long. I enjoy mixing up creative vegan baked recipes as well as animal-free herbal products."

Ingredients

1 1/2 cups flour
3 ounces silken tofu
1/4 cup olive oil
2 teaspoons almond oil
1/2 teaspoon baking powder
3/4 cup brown sugar

1/2 teaspoon cinnamon

1 teaspoon ginger

dried cranberries

Directions

Preheat oven to 350. Combine tofu, oil, sugar, and seasonings into a mixing bowl.

Add in the rest of ingredients until it forms a dough-like mix.

Form into small balls and place onto greased pan. Bake for 10-12 minutes.

Magickal Notes

David shares his magickal uses for these cookies:

"Mostly listed in the content itself but in terms of specific correspondences, cranberries are related to the sun and mars. Cinnamon and ginger have both solar and earthen correspondences, which add a great seasonal flare to its meaning.

"These bitterly sweet cookies make a perfect snack for your Yule festivities. The cranberries align your energies to the growing strength of the sun and even look like tiny suns nestled in the cookies themselves. Cranberries are famous for being able to grow in areas that would otherwise be considered wasteland. When we eat food with cranberries, we're bringing in a "survivor" energy that helps sustain us for the raging winter months to come."

Grandma Olson's Kringle

Submitted by Erik Olson

So many of us love sweets during the Winter holiday season. It seems that traditions of holiday baking are far reaching. Erik brings us traditional sweets (or not so sweets) from Norway.

Erik says:

"The winter holidays are very special in the Scandinavian countries. With the Christianization of Norway, Christmas became the most important holiday at the dark of the year. The Norwegian word for Christmas is Jul, pronounced almost exactly the same as how we say Yule. This cookie is one that I grew up eating at the winter holiday. I share with you two variations on Kringle, my grandmother's version and the updated version that I use. Kringle is traditionally shaped into a figure eight. I like to think of them as infinity symbols. Whichever shape you see, they are traditionally eaten plain, topped with a smear of unsalted butter, or dipped in the hot beverage of your choice."

"One thing to be aware of if you attempt to make my grandmother's recipe, there is no amount of flour defined in the recipe other than the phrase "enough flour to knead 'good.'" Let your intuition and cooking experience guide you when determining how much flour that is."

Ingredients

1 cup sugar
Pinch of salt
1 heaping Tablespoon shortening (Crisco or the like)
1 teaspoon baking soda
1 egg
1 teaspoon vanilla
Dash of nutmeg

1 cup sour cream

Directions

Mix all ingredients in the order in which they are listed above, then add enough flour to knead "good." (start with 1/4 cup and go from there) Make a roll. Cut pieces off with a knife. Roll each piece about 10 inches long on board with very little flour. Make figure eight. Place on un-greased cookie sheet and bake in 400°F oven until lightly brown.

Erik Olson's Kringle

"This recipe is large enough to make about 100 cookies, depending on the size you roll your dough. Also, this is a fairly soft dough. It is best to refrigerate the unused portions to firm the dough up while it is waiting to be worked"

Ingredients

1 stick butter (unsalted)

5 cups cake flour

1 cup plain flour

1 tbsp baking soda

2 cups sugar

1/2 teaspoon salt

2 teaspoon vanilla

2 eggs (large)

2 cups sour cream

Directions

Combine cake flour and plain flour in a large mixing bowl. Add the baking soda and mix together with a whisk. Cut the butter into eight or more portions and blend with the flour. Work the butter and flour together until no pieces of butter are larger than a small pea.

Combine sugar, salt, vanilla, and eggs together. Beat mixture until completely blended. Add sour cream and continue to beat until well mixed and consistent in color.

Combine all ingredients and work together until the dough begins to take shape. The dough will be quite soft and sticky. Incorporate up to an additional half-cup of flour to make the dough a workable consistency.

Split the dough into two halves and refrigerate for approximately 20 minutes to allow the dough to firm up. While dough is chilling, pre-heat oven to 375 degrees and line a baking sheet with a piece of baking parchment.

Take first half of dough out of refrigerator. Working on a lightly floured surface, roll dough into a thick log approximately one-and-a-half inches in diameter. Cut half-inch pieces off of this log and roll the cut piece into a long thin rope of dough, as thin as a pencil or a little thicker if you prefer. You want the dough rope to wind up being between six and eight inches long.

Once you have rolled the dough rope, bring the two ends of the rope together to form an oval. Cross one side of the oval over the other to make a figure eight, making sure the seam where the ends of the rope meet is on the underside. Transfer shaped dough onto baking sheet. You may find it is easier to shape the dough on the cookie sheet after you have rolled the dough rope. Don't overcrowd the figure eights as this dough has a tendency to expand a fair amount. Once you have filled your baking sheet with figure eight shapes, bake the kringle for approximately ten minutes. Do not let the dough cook longer than slightly tan on top. Ideally, the baked cookies should still be pale on top even when completely cooked.

These cookies have a soft texture that is more similar to a cake's consistency than the crisp quality one often associates with cookies.

Magickal Notes

The ingredients in these cookies are fairly simple. They are the basis of many cookies and cakes we see throughout this chapter and in other cookbooks alike. What makes these special is the shape they are rolled into. The shape of an infinite symbol is very sacred. The symbol of "forever" or "never ending" can be applied to whatever emotion you choose; never ending joy, happiness, health, balance. While making these infinity symbols, with each one have a clear intention of what you want to put in them and bless them with your positive thoughts and energy.

Chapter 7:
Magickal Smorgasbord

"One of the nicest things about life is the way we must regularly stop whatever it is we are doing and devote our attention to eating."

– Luciano Pavarotti

Leftovers are sometimes the best part of cooking! On a Friday night, we often sit around the table with one plate of spaghetti, one bowl of chili, a bit of potatoes and a restaurant container with half of a NY Strip steak. Everyone gets what they are in the mood for and nothing goes to waste. This section is like those wonderful leftovers. These are the fun, different, and unique recipes that needed a chapter all their own.

Think of all the wonderful potluck dinners or cookouts you have been to. No two dishes are ever the same. For that fact, no two potlucks are ever the same. Some people may have their signature dish that graces the table every time, but still, it is never the same twice. That is because cooking is an art. You don't have to be a Michelangelo to draw and you don't need to be Julia Child to cook a great meal. A good cook is not someone who cooks a fancy meal every night or whips up liver pâté for fun, but is someone who loves what they are doing. Likewise, good Kitchen Magick comes from the heart, not the gourmet food store.

A good friend of mine always says she and I could cook up the same meal with the same ingredients and they would taste completely different. She is right. Magickal cooking has more to do with the way you feel when you are cooking than it does with the ingredients you are actually using. Yes, of course, the fresher the ingredients the better, but if your energy and intention is off, or worse, negative, then it will not matter what you are cooking. At first thought this chapter was meant to focus on special dietary needs, but it has grown to include everything from vegan "chicken" soup to food for your dog familiar. Take a look through the smorgasbord we've assembled in this chapter. You might be surprised what you find!

Oven Baked Ratatouille

I sent this recipe around on my mailing last year during late summer and it got rave reviews. It is really easy and makes a ton, so there will be plenty of leftovers! This easy Ratatouille celebrates the best of early Fall or late Summer veggies and it is gluten-free and vegan (depending of course on what you serve with it). These ingredients should be in abundance at your farmers market from August right though early October.

Ingredients

1/2 cup Cucina Aurora Rosemary Olive Oil

2 onions, cut into wedges

6 cloves garlic, minced

2 zucchini, cut into rounds

1 eggplant, cut into bite size cubes

1 summer squash or yellow zucchini

3 fresh tomatoes, cut into wedges

1 8oz. can no salt added tomato sauce

Chopped fresh rosemary, sage, and parsley to taste

Sea salt and coarse ground pepper to taste

Directions

Preheat oven to 400. In a large sauce pan, heat oil. Add the garlic and onions and cook about 5 min or until soft. Add zucchini, eggplant, and squash and cook until just tender, about 10-15 minutes or when vegetable start to sizzle. Add herbs and tomato sauce, salt and pepper. Remove from heat and transfer to oven safe casserole. Cover and bake in hot oven about 2 hours, stirring occasionally so that the veggies do not burn. Serve on a slice of Italian bread sprinkled with grated Romano cheese, serve over pasta for a primavera dish, or just eat alongside your favorite meal!

Magickal Notes

The ritual here is to take your time in choosing your veggies. Pick the ones that feel right to you. As you chop the ingredients remember the powers these foods hold, onion banishes negativity, garlic protects, zucchini is a food of the God and eggplant of the Goddess. While this dish cooks down in the oven, light an orange or yellow candle for joy and positive energy. Now is the time of year to reap what we have sewn. The harvest season comes so we can prepare for the long winter months ahead. As you light your candle think on all the hard work you have done these past summer months and draw to you the good you deserve, should it be for the good of all.

Ancient Grains Sausage and Lentils

This dish is a bit different from your everyday meal. It simple and hearty with easy to find ingredients, but when I tell people about it they always say something along the line of "Wow, I never thought to put those things together!" A very quick sauté of chicken sausage, onions, and sage mixed with ready to eat cooked lentils served over quinoa (keen-wah) will be a new family favorite. You can make this dish vegetarian by replacing the chicken sausage with a suitable substitute.

Ingredients

1 package Italian-style chicken sausage, sliced into bite sided rounds

1 large onion, chopped

3 cloves garlic, minced

1/4 cup fresh sage

2 Tablespoons fresh parsley (or one Tablespoon dried)

1 teaspoon ground black pepper (more to taste)

2 Tablespoons olive oil

1 package ready to eat vacuumed packed lentils

2 cups fresh sliced mushrooms (optional)

Pinch sea salt

1 cup dry Quinoa

Grated Romano cheese

Directions

In a medium sauce pan, cook quinoa to package instructions. In a large skillet, heat oil. Add onions, and garlic and cook until just softened, about 3 minutes. Add the sausage, sage, parsley, black pepper (and mushrooms, if desired) and salt. Cook until the vegetables are softened and the sausage is browned. Add the lentils and continue cooking another 5 minutes until lentils are heated though. Make a bed of cooked Quinoa in the center of a plate and serve the sausage mixture on top of it. Sprinkle with Romano cheese and fresh cracked black pepper. Serve hot.

Magickal Notes

Quinoa is an ancient food from South America. The Incas held it in the highest regard as a sacred food, called "the Mother of all Grains". Quinoa is actually not a grain, but a seed. It cooks up just like rice, has tons of protein and is gluten-free. Quinoa still holds its magickal ancient powers. This food has been around for thousands of years and is as sacred now as it was then. Quinoa's energy is that of protection and nurturing. Quinoa also helps us to stay connected to the Earth spirits and Mother Goddess. Combining that energy with the properties of the lentils in this meal brings peace and contentment. Leave one spoonful of this dish out in the yard as an offering to the Great Mother Goddess and all she gives us.

Butternut Squash Risotto

3 Tablespoons butter

2 Tablespoons minced fresh sage

1 Tablespoon minced fresh parsley

1 Tablespoon minced fresh rosemary

6 cups water

2 cups pureed butternut squash

3 Tablespoons olive oil

1 large sweet Vidalia onion, sliced thin

2 cups Arborio rice

½ cup white wine

½ cup smoked Gouda cheese, shredded

½ cup grated Romano cheese

Salt and pepper to taste

Directions

In a skillet heat 1 Tablespoon butter and 1 Tablespoon olive oil. Add onions. Cook, stirring constantly, until golden brown and caramelized, but do not burn. Set aside. In a large bowl, whisk together squash puree and water. Set aside. In a large sauce pan heat 2 Tablespoons olive oil and 2 Tablespoons butter until butter is melted. Add the caramelized onions and rice, and stir to coat all rice in butter and oil. Add the sage, parsley, and rosemary. Add in the wine until it is complexly absorbed. One cupful at a time, add in the water and puree mixture. Stirring constantly and not adding any more liquid until completely absorbed. After all liquid is absorbed and rice is tender add in cheeses, salt, and pepper. Remove form heat and let stand 2-5 minutes. Serve warm.

Magickal Notes

Risotto is the best friend of any one with a Gluten allergy. It is creamy and pasta-like, but free of any and all wheat products! What is really fantastic about this super absorbent rice grain is that is carries all the same magickal properties of other rice. Rice is a food associated with abundant blessings. Rice helps us to grow and see the blessings around us even when they are difficult to see. This little grain has qualities properties as well. Risotto, unlike other rice, requires much attention. You must tend to it and never let it sit more than a moment without stirring or it will burn. Similarly in our lives we must constantly be in motion towards a better self, and actively grateful for our abundant blessings or we, too, can get burned. While stirring this risotto, diligently keep in mind all the blessings you have and what abundance you live in everyday. Fill your pot with gratitude and joy and you will bring more of the same into your life.

Chewy Chocolate Chip Cookies

On occasion I have been asked to provide food for the Temple of Witchcraft events. I make tons of sandwiches, salads and wraps and rely on volunteers to help me take the orders, and distribute the food. Since I love sweets, I could not help myself when getting to make huge double size cookies for everyone to enjoy as they shopped the vending tables at Beltane and TempleFest celebrations. This is the recipe everyone loves, that sells out before lunch time and no one ever believes is free of Gluten, nuts, wheat, refined sugar, and eggs! This recipe fought its way into this section instead of the "Sweets" chapter because it is a perfect Gluten Free cookie recipe.

Ingredients

1 cup all purpose gluten free flour

1 cup garbanzo bean flour

1/4 cup flax meal

1 1/4 cup organic evaporated cane juice

1 teaspoon salt

1 1/2 teaspoon baking soda

1 1/2 teaspoon Xanthium gum

1 teaspoon cinnamon

1/3 cup apple sauce

1 cup butter, softened

1 Tablespoon vanilla extract

1 cup chocolate chips

Directions

Preheat oven to 325 degrees. In a large bowl combine flours, flax meal, cane juice, salt, baking soda, Xanthium gum, and cinnamon. Mix together until well combined. Add in the apple sauce, butter, and vanilla. Mix well until all butter is evenly dispersed. Batter will be very stiff. Add in chocolate chips. Drop by rounded Tablespoon full (use a teaspoon for smaller cookies) on to un-greased cookie sheet. Be sure to leave enough room for cookies to spread. Bake, one cookie sheet at a time, for 14 minutes. Remove to wire rack and cool.

Magickal Notes

Although the ingredients are different then in typical chocolate chip cookies, the magickal property of the end result is the same. A warm, chewy piece of heaven, and you can share them with picky cookie eaters who would never know the difference! Chocolate is a love food, and when baked into these soft cookies, reminds us of being loved and cared for as a child. Baking up a bunch of these cookies is an age old way of showing love and affection.

"Happy Hound" Chien Cuisine

Submitted by Alaric Albertsson, Mars, PA

There is magic in *all* the food we prepare, no matter for our human or animal family members. Anyone who has had the joy of sharing their life with an animal companion truly knows how important can be.

Alaric says:

"I grew up with dogs, and have had dogs throughout my adult life. For me, they truly are familiar spirits. My dogs are not locked away during group rituals, but are taught to accompany us and keep out from underfoot. I currently share my life with one elderly female, Lucky, a mixed breed who is now in her mid-teens.

"I became aware of the potential health challenges of commercial dog food when one of my own dogs developed a chronic skin condition. Most commercial preparations include corn and soy because these grains are cheap, but they also cause allergic reactions in many dogs.

"If your dog familiar has been living on dry kibble, begin feeding a 50/50 mix of Chien Cuisine and kibble and gradually reduce the kibble until he or she adjusts to eating real food. Instantly changing the dog's diet to Chien Cuisine can result in diarrhea or vomiting, just as would happen if you were to eat a healthy salad after subsisting for years on nothing but Big Macs™ and fries."

"Don't be surprised if you see an improvement in your dog's coat, cleaner ears, and a notable decrease in "doggy odor" within a week or two after switching your dog to real food."

Ingredients

3-4 pounds ground meat (turkey, chicken, lamb or lean beef)

1 cup brown rice

6-9 carrots, chopped fine

1 medium sized yam or sweet potato, chopped into small
bite size pieces

2 small yellow squash or zucchini, sliced

1 can of peas, drained

3 Tablespoons flax oil (or canola oil)

Directions

Brown the meat in a large skillet. While meat is browning, in a large pot combine 2 cups water, carrots, and sweet potatoes. Add rice and boil. Reduce heat and simmer for 30 minutes, stirring occasionally. When meat is browned, drain off any extra fat/grease. Add squash/zucchini and peas to the veggie/rice mix and continue simmering another 10 minutes. Mix together the meat, the veggie/rice mix and flax oil in a large bowl. Serve portions appropriate for the dog's size (two cups a day – one for breakfast and one for dinner.) Refrigerate for up to a week in an air tight container.

Magickal Notes

Use this recipe to celebrate and thank your furry companion for the gift of unconditional love; that tail wagging when you come home from a long day or the friendly nudge of your arm that says "Pet Me". While preparing this feast, call upon Diana or Hecate, to whom Dogs are sacred, and ask them to bless your beloved friend.

Chapter Seven: Magickal Smorgasbord

Blaze's Crock-pot Shrimp Creole

Submitted by Gail Wood, Freeville, NY

This recipe could have fit right into our Witchy Entertaining section or Pantry Magick because it is easy, feeds many, and is made with simple ingredients. But we put it in this chapter because it really has a life of its own. Made in the crock pot and cooked up to Creole perfection this dish is a new and delicious way to eat shrimp.

Gail says:

"One of the more common nutritional myths is that shrimp need to be shunned because they are a source of bad cholesterol. This myth has not only been disproven, but this delicious fresh and salt water crustacean is nutritionally beneficial as a source of omega-3 fatty acids, B-12 and niacin. Shrimp is rich in the minerals of iron, zinc and copper."

Ingredients

1 1/2 cup chopped onions

3/4 cup chopped celery

1 clove garlic, minced

1 28-ounce can whole tomatoes

2 8-ounce cans tomato sauce

1 teaspoon salt

1 teaspoon sugar

1/4 teaspoon paprika

3-6 drops Tabasco Sauce

1 pound fresh shrimp or 16-ounce package frozen shelled shrimp, rinsed and drained

Directions

Combine all ingredients except shrimp in the Crock-pot and stir to blend well. Cover and cook on low for 7-9 hours (high for 3-4 hours). During the last hour, turn the Crock-pot to high, add shrimp, and cook for one hour or until the shrimp is pink.

Magickal Notes

Like many other creatures from the sea, shrimp are of Aphrodite, Goddess of Love, passion, and love-making. Aphrodite was born of the sea, and so all of the sea's creatures are hers.

Gail offers some more information on the magickal properties of shrimp as she uses them:

"In the web of life, shrimp are tiny creatures that help maintain a healthy ecosystem by preventing algae build-up in an aquarium or underwater living space and by getting rid of debris. As we consume shrimp, we can imagine it magically preventing a build-up of harmful blockages and debris in our systems. The tasty combination of vegetables and spices in this Creole dish remind us life is not only to be lived beneficially but also enjoyed for all the spice it can give us!"

Winter Solstice Saffron Bread in Braided Rounds

Submitted by Ruby Sara, Chicago, IL

Bread baking is truly magickal. It takes patience and caring. Kneading and rolling out dough you really put so much of yourself into the food. This bread takes the better part of a day to make. Like most risen breads there is a lot of waiting involved, but the reward is worth it

Ruby says:

"These rounds are perfect for holiday parties and solstice gatherings. They are warm, yellowy, and sweet, and the added beauty of the braiding makes them almost too lovely to eat (though I recommend eating them, because they are delicious). This recipe makes 2 loaves."

Ingredients

1 Tablespoon yeast (instant or active dry)
1/4 teaspoon saffron threads
1-3/4 cups hot water (120 degrees F)
1/2 cup sugar
1 Tablespoon salt
6-1/2 to 7 cups white flour
4 large eggs at room temperature, lightly beaten
1/2 cup vegetable oil or butter
1-1/2 Tablespoons vanilla extract
Handful of golden raisins (optional)

For the Glaze
1 large egg yolk
1 teaspoon vanilla extract
1/2 teaspoon sugar

Directions

In a large bowl combine the yeast, sugar, salt, and 2 cups of the flour. Crush the saffron threads in your hand, and add them to the hot water and allow it to sit for a few minutes in a small bowl. Add the saffron water (should still be hot), eggs, oil, and vanilla. Beat with an electric mixer on high until smooth. Add the remaining flour, 1/2 cup at a time. Continue beating until the dough is too stiff to stir. Turn out on a lightly floured surface and knead until smooth and elastic, about 4 minutes. Place the dough in a greased container (the container should be fairly deep, as the dough will rise quite a lot). Turn the dough once to coat the top and cover. Let rise at room temperature until doubled in bulk, approx. 1-1/2 to 2 hours, though times may be longer or shorter depending on the temperature in your kitchen.

Grease or parchment-line two baking sheets. Gently deflate the dough. Turn the dough onto a lightly oiled or floured surface (the use of oil versus flour depends on whether your dough is more wet or dry at this point, though braiding is easier using oil, as the dough sticks less to your hands and there is less chance of it drying out in the process). Divide into 8 equal portions and roll into balls. Braid your dough into 2 rounds (see braiding instructions following), and place on baking sheets. Cover loosely and allow to rise until nearly doubled in bulk, about 30-40 minutes.

Twenty minutes before baking, preheat the oven to 350F. To make the vanilla egg glaze, whisk together the egg yolk, vanilla, and sugar in a small bowl. Beat until well blended. Gently brush the dough surfaces with a thick layer of the glaze. Place the baking sheet(s) on a rack in the center of the oven and bake 40-45 minutes, or until a deep, golden brown and the loaves sound hollow when tapped with your finger. Carefully lift the loaves off the baking sheet(s) with a spatula and transfer to cooling racks. Cool completely before slicing.

Braiding Rounds

Roll out each ball of dough with a rolling pin into a rectangle. At this point, if you wish, add a small scattering of golden raisins and roll them up into each piece of dough.

Roll each piece up into logs lengthwise towards you and set them aside for 10 minutes on your work table, preferably under cover so they don't dry out. They will have risen somewhat.

Take your risen dough strands and roll them out with your hands, gently, making them as long as possible. Do this with four pieces of dough until they are all about the same length. Lay the pieces out in front of you, tic-tac-toe style.

Each strand should be placed in opposite directions; one side is over/under, the next row is then under/over. There should now be 4 sets of 2 strands each coming out from the four sides of the woven middle, one under and one over in each set.

From each set, pick up the one that was "under" and pull it over its partner, thereby placing each of these "unders" over their corresponding partner, in a deosil rotation. Practically speaking, this means that the left piece of each set will be placed over the right piece of each set.

When this rotation is done, work in the opposite direction, widdershins. What was formerly the right piece, will now go over the left piece in the counter-clockwise direction; the pieces are not yet next to each other as they are still apart from the first rotation; pull them close to each other and bring the right piece, i.e. the one you did not touch in the first rotation, over the left piece of the neighboring strand.

After this second rotation is done, do a third one, now going back in the other direction.

Do one more opposite rotation if you have enough dough left.

To finish, pinch each set of two ends together firmly, then bring all four sets together towards the center.

Now carefully flip over and look – when done correctly, you'll see a beautifully braided round in your hand!

Magickal Notes

Rare and expensive saffron, with its burnt orange color and distinctive taste, has been used for years to lift spirits and please the pallet. A pinch of saffron baked into braided bread is the perfect way to celebrate the Sun God at Yule or any other time of year you wish to honor him.

Flour-less Peanut Butter Cookie Drops

Submitted by Matooka Moonbear, Manchester, NH

This recipe proves how simple, wholesome ingredients can make a delicious treat. Nothing complicated in Matooka's recipe. This recipe is completely gluten-free and perfectly wonderful. Try mixing in a handful of chocolate chips or even raisins for a variation.

Ingredients

1 cup peanut butter

¾ cup brown sugar

1 egg

1 tsp vanilla

Directions

Preheat oven to 350 degrees. In a large bowl, mix peanut butter, brown sugar, egg and vanilla. Line a cookie sheet with parchment paper. Drop peanut butter dough by rounded teaspoon full on to the prepared baking sheet being sure to leave room for cookies to spread. Bake for 8-10 minutes or until golden brown.

Magickal Notes

As we have seen throughout this book, peanut butter is a favorite of many. It can be made into cookies, cakes, brownies, even stir fries and marinates. This cookie recipe is different than most because it is flour-less. There is no magickal energy here stronger then the prosperity of the peanut butter. The egg helps to bind the peanut butter together with growth and fertility energy, making these cookies a great treat to share for any wealth or growth rituals.

Chapter Seven: Magickal Smorgasbord

Stag God Venison

Submitted by Wren MacGowen

Not many people eat venison in middle-class suburbia. I grew up on it and so I was thrilled when Wren submitted this recipe. My father was a hunter and every November we would get a freezer full of tender meat that would last us through the winter. I used to love frying up some venison cutlets with just a little olive oil and a side of mashed potatoes on a cold winter night. The meat is tender and only slightly gamey to give it a very distinctive flavor. If you are not a hunter you can find venison and some local organic or natural markets.

Ingredients

1 lb. venison medallions or cutlets

2 Tablespoons mustard (your favorite kind)

1/2 cup bread crumbs

1/4 cup very finely chopped nuts (walnuts, almonds, or pecans)

1 teaspoon black pepper

1 Tablespoon garlic powder

1 Tablespoon onion powder

1 teaspoon salt

1 teaspoon steak seasoning to taste

3 Tablespoons olive oil

Directions

Marinate venison in mustard (mix venison in mustard and allow to stand for at least 15 minutes). While venison is marinating, mix bread crumbs, nuts, and spices in a container suitable to coat the venison in. Heat olive oil in a heavy skillet, you will need enough to brown and cook the venison. While skillet is heating, evenly coat marinated venison pieces with the breadcrumb mixture. When skillet has thoroughly heated, brown and cook venison until desired doneness, about 10 -15 minutes. Make sure to brown on all sides. Gravy can be made from pan drippings and served over the venison.

Magickal Notes

Some cultures believe that when you eat the flesh of an animal you take in its spirit, knowledge, and in some cases, its power. This is true of Food Magick. Although most of us don't really feel that way about our chicken nuggets, or beef jerky, we are in fact, taking in the energy of these animals. When eating venison, we partake in the wisdom, power, and strength of the Stag or Horned God. Celebrate him by honoring the deer. Be mindful when making this dish, as well as all others where an animal has given its life so you can live, to come from a place of gratitude and wonder.

Whole Wheat Vegan Bread

Submitted by Jocelyn VanBokkelen

There is a lack of bread baking done at home these days. It is time consuming but, I think, well worth it. This bread is Jocelyn's own adaptation of an old recipe. She has revamped it to make it vegan and uses whole wheat flour and flax meal for extra nutritional value.

Jocelyn says:

"In the Beginning, there was only bread baked at home. At least it was when my mother-in-law was growing up on a small dairy farm in the 1920s. I live on that dairy farm now, except there hasn't been an actual dairy cow here since 1927, when industrial agriculture started to grow and made it more economical for these folks to go back to being teachers. In the 1960s my mother-in-law went down to the bakery to buy fresh bread for her family, until the bakery closed in 1966. About then, what was available for bread at the grocery store was sliced white bread. My mother in law went back to baking the bread of her youth. When it became necessary for her to work, her son, now my husband, took over the family baking. I use this same recipe now, and have learned to modify it to suit the audience."

Ingredients

3 cups whole wheat flour

2 packets of yeast

1/2 cup hot water

3 Tablespoons ground flax meal

4 Tablespoons honey

3 Tablespoons olive oil

½ teaspoon salt

2 cups boiling water

Directions

Dissolve yeast in water, set aside. Place honey, olive oil, and salt into a large mixing bowl

Add boiling water to honey mixture, stir until dissolved. Add flour and flax meal and mix. Add yeast mixture and mix. Continue adding flour and mixing until it is of kneading consistency and knead, adding flour as necessary until it is smooth. Set in a greased bowl and let rise until doubled (1-3 hours). Turn out of bowl onto a floured surface, break into two even pieces and knead each piece. Form into loaves, placing them in greased bread pans, or on a greased cookie sheet for a round loaf. Preheat oven to 350 degrees. Let bread rise until doubled again. Bake at 350 degrees for 45 minutes.

Perfect Paella

Submitted by Allura, Salem, MA

Paella is a traditional rice dish originating in Spain. It can be made with different types of seafood, chicken or even duck and rabbit. In this Paella, Allura uses Arborio rice, usually associated with Italian risotto, in place of regular white rice. There is also a mixture of sausage, seafood, and chicken, making this almost like a Jambalaya.

Ingredients

1 lb. mild or hot sausages, sliced (or use Chorizo)
1 lb. shrimp, cleaned & deveined
10 small clams, cleaned (or use mussels)
1 medium onion, chopped
2 cloves garlic, minced
2 peppers, red & green, sliced thin
1 large tomato, peeled & chopped
Salt & pepper to taste
6 chicken thighs (salt before cooking)
1 1/2cups Arborio rice
1/4 teaspoon crushed saffron threads
3 3/4 cups chicken broth
1/2 cup frozen peas
1 tsp olive oil

Directions

Heat oil in a large frying pan over medium heat. Add sausage & cook until no longer pink, remove to paper towels to drain. Brown chicken on all sides in same pan drippings about 15 minutes, remove. Add onion, peppers, 1 teaspoon salt & 1/4 teaspoon pepper, cook until soft

Add tomatoes and cook 5 minutes more. Place veggie mixture, rice, saffron & chicken stock in pan, mix well. Add chicken & clams to rice & top with sausages & peas. Bring to a boil over medium-high heat on top of stove. Put into pre-heated oven and bake, uncovered about 35-40 minutes. After 15 minutes, add shrimp & continue cooking until liquid is absorbed.

Remove, cover tightly with lid or foil. Let stand 10 minutes before serving.

Magickal Notes

There are so many wonderful ingredients in this dish it is hard to narrow down its magickal properties. Chicken is a good health and well-being food, where the sea food holds love and passionate qualities. The sausage brings a bit of zest and adventurous energy into the mix and the saffron pulls in the Sun energy. To me the combination of all these ingredients held together by the rice makes this dish a magickal way of combining things that normally don't go together. Make this dish when introducing people. Allow the energies of Earth (rice) Air (chicken) Fire(peppers and saffron) and Water (seafood) join together and bring harmony to the table.

Crust-less Spinach Quiche

Beth Moondragon, Ayre, MA

I love, love, *love* quiche! It's like a giant omelet in a pie crust. How wonderful is that? Here Beth has shared a very special crust-less quiche with pesto. Having no crust means it is great for people with wheat or gluten allergies.

Beth says:

"The spinach quiche is made special by adding pesto. I make my own fresh pesto, which makes it even more yummy. This is a family favorite, a great way to get the kids to eat spinach, and it's easy because there's no crust."

Ingredients

2 cups shredded mozzarella cheese

1/2 cup whipping (heavy) cream

1/3 cup Pesto

1 package (10 ounces) frozen chopped spinach, thawed and
  squeezed to drain

5 eggs

1 cup chunky tomato sauce (optional)

Directions

Heat the oven to 375 degrees. Spray a 9-inch pie plate, 1.5 inches deep, with nonstick cooking spray.

Mix 1 1/2 cups of the cheese, with the whipping cream, pesto, spinach, and eggs until well blended; pour in quiche dish. Bake 25-30 minutes or until knife inserted in center comes out clean. Sprinkle with remaining 1/2 cup cheese. Bake 2-3 minutes or until cheese is melted. Meanwhile, heat tomato sauce in a small saucepan until hot; keep warm. To serve, cut quiche into wedges. Serve with tomato sauce.

Magickal Notes

Spinach is the kind of food I could eat all the time. Just talking about it makes me want to go out to the local farm and pick up a huge bushel to cook up with some garlic and olive oil for dinner tonight. This quiche features spinach alongside pesto. Pesto is a paste made from fresh basil, olive oil, garlic, and sometimes pine nuts. Both spinach and basil are money foods. Although basil has other attributes as well, like love, I use it mostly as a money drawing food. While mixing all these ingredients together envision your money growing and growing. Use these green vegetables to bring more money into your life, that it harm none of course.

Veggie Shepherd's Pie
Submitted by Jeffery Snow

Shepherd's pie is a favorite in my home. It is usually made with beef and/or lamb covered in mashed potatoes and baked until steaming hot. But this dish can be a real downer if you are a vegetarian. Never fear! Jeffery has provided us with a great recipe for a new vegetarian twist on this old classic. Just as warm and comforting as the original, but tons of veggies and no meat!

Jeffery says:

"I hope you like it. It is a staple at Shadow Wood, even our carnivorous members love it!"

Ingredients

6 medium Yukon gold potatoes, peeled and diced

Pinch Kosher salt

2 Tablespoons extra-virgin olive oil

1 large red onion

3 large carrots, chopped

2 stalks celery, chopped

4 small turnips, chopped

6 cloves garlic, minced

Freshly ground pepper

1/2 bunch fresh parsley, leaves chopped (save stems)

1 1/2 Tablespoons Worcestershire sauce or A-1 steak sauce

5 Tablespoons unsalted butter

1 package vegetarian protein crumbles (such as
   Morningstar Farms)

2/3 cup milk or half-and-half

Directions

Cover the potatoes with water in a pot, add sea salt, cover, and boil until the potatoes are fork-tender, 25 minutes. Meanwhile, heat the oil in a stove top casserole dish or shallow enamel pot over medium-high heat. Add the onion, carrots, celery, turnips, and garlic. Season with salt and pepper and cook until the vegetables brown, 8 minutes. Add 1 1/2 cups cooking liquid from the potatoes to the casserole dish. Lower the heat and scrape up any browned bits with a wooden spoon. Tie the parsley stems with twine and add to the pot. Cover and simmer until the vegetables are tender. Stir in the Worcestershire sauce, 2 Tablespoons butter and the veggie crumbles, 5 minutes. Remove the parsley stems and stir in the chopped parsley. Keep warm.

Drain the potatoes and mash with the remaining 3 Tablespoons butter and the milk; season with salt and pepper and spoon over the casserole. Sprinkle with Parmesan, if desired. Broil until golden brown, 5 minutes.

Magickal Notes

It is no wonder Jeffery's friends never miss the meat in this shepherd's pie. This dish is a very grounding one. Potatoes, turnips, carrots and even onions are all root vegetables. These foods help us to stay grounded, focused and rooted in our lives. They help us to reconnect with Earth and our own spirit. This dish will bring you back when you have been floating about and can't seem to get your footing back, metaphorically and literally.

Vegan Chicken Noodle Soup

Submitted by Eric Staunton

Ingredients

8 oz. elbow pasta

12 oz. Morningstar Meal Starters "chicken" strips (or other vegan faux chicken)

2-3 carrots, peeled and cut into bite sized pieces

1/2 small onion, diced

2 stalks celery, cut into ~1/8 inch pieces

2 Tablespoons salt free poultry seasoning

6 cups vegetable stock

Oil as needed

Directions

Cook pasta according to package directions, rinse in cold water and set aside. Brown faux chicken strips in oil, cut into bite-sized pieces and set aside. In heavy bottomed pot, sauté carrot, onion and celery until vegetables are tender. Add seasoning and stock, bring to a boil. Add pasta and faux chicken pieces and cook until heated through. Taste and adjust seasonings as desired. Serve hot.

Magickal Notes

When making a dish like chicken soup the key is intention. Intention is paramount in all magickal works, but especially in Kitchen and Food Magick. Whatever we put into the food we take into our selves. Since soup is something we usually only make when we are feeling under the weather it is important that intentions are clear. Stir this soup clockwise and fill it with healing energy. Pour light and love from your heart center though your hand into the spoon and into the soup. Be sure that when taking a serving you take only what you can finish.

Do not throw away any unfinished soup. For this type of magick to work you must think of it as a potion and take every last drop.

Chapter Seven: Magickal Smorgasbord

About the Author

Dawn Aurora Hunt—known as "the Kitchen Witch"—is the founder of Cucina Aurora Kitchen Witchery. She teaches classes on Kitchen Witchery and food Magic, touring and giving workshops along the East Coast. Creating the sacred every day though simple spell recipes and kitchen rituals, Dawn has brought food Magick into the homes of Pagans and Non-Pagans alike. Through her line of infused olive oils, dips, cookie mixes, and Kitchen Witch Ware products she has shown that simple home-made foods are best for the body, mind and soul. She and her husband, Justin, live in the Merrimack Valley in Massachusetts. For more information visit her website: *www.cucinaaurora.com* and follow her on Facebook and Twitter at Cucina Aurora Kitchen Witchery.

The Temple of Witchcraft
MYSTERY SCHOOL AND SEMINARY

Witchcraft is a tradition of experience, and the best way to experience the path of the Witch is to actively train in its magickal and spiritual lessons. The Temple of Witchcraft provides a complete system of training and tradition, with four degrees found in the Mystery School for personal and magickal development and a fifth degree in the Seminary for the training of High Priestesses and High Priests interested in serving the gods, spirits, and community as ministers. Teachings are divided by degree into the Oracular, Fertility, Ecstatic, Gnostic, and Resurrection Mysteries. Training emphasizes the ability to look within, awaken your own gifts and abilities, and perform both lesser and greater magicks for your own evolution and the betterment of the world around you. The Temple of Witchcraft offers both in-person and online courses with direct teaching and mentorship. Classes use the *Temple of Witchcraft* series of books and CD Companions as primary texts, supplemented monthly with information from the Temple's Book of Shadows, MP3 recordings of lectures and meditations from our founders, social support through group discussion with classmates, and direct individual feedback from a mentor.

For more information and current schedules, please visit: *www.templeofwitchcraft.org.*

CPSIA information can be obtained at www.ICGtesting.com
Printed in the USA
BVOW020835050112

279577BV00005BB/2/P

9 780982 774328